C000199187

ABOUT ETON

BY ADAM NICOLSON
& ERIC ANDERSON

LONG BARN BOOKS

CONTENTS

ILLUSTRATIONS

MATT MOWBRAY
with additional photographs from
Eton College Collections and Photographic Archive,
Getty Images, Ian Macdonald and Philip Bermingham.

ACKNOWLEDGEMENTS AND
FURTHER READING

The authors gratefully acknowledge the help given them by innumerable conversations with boys, Old Etonians and masters. They are also indebted to those who helped their research or read parts of the book in typescript, especially William Waldegrave, Andrew Gailey, Tony Little, Andrew Wynn, Michael Meredith, Matthew Rice, Tony Jarvis, Penny Hatfield, Henrietta Ryan, Bill O'Hearn, Christine Vickers, Rachel Bond and Katie Lord. Matthew Mowbray took many of the photographs of contemporary Eton for us and Ian Macdonald and Philip Bermingham generously gave permission to use their photograph of the chapel and library. Peter Wilkinson drew the map. Susan Hill and Julie Martin, our publisher and designer, were unfailingly efficient and kind.

The best books to read if you are interested in the history and buildings of Eton are
H.C.Maxwell-Lyte, *A History of Eton College*, 4th ed. 1911, Macmillan
Tim Card, *Eton Established* and *Eton Renewed*, 2001 and 1994, John Murray
J.C.Austen-Leigh, *The Eton Guide*, periodically revised, available on the Eton College Website.

For Poppy

FOREWORD

BY TONY LITTLE,
HEAD MASTER OF ETON

THERE HAVE BEEN MANY BOOKS written about Eton over the centuries, many of them rather arid histories of an institution, others partial personal accounts, more self-justification than observation. There have been few attempts to capture the spirit of the place, fewer still that have come near the mark. This short book, written by two people who have a wryly critical affection for Eton, fills the gap.

To the outside world, the word Eton conjures up all manner of images to different people – and it always has. To some, 'Eton' is shorthand for privilege, arrogance and a very lofty view of the world. This book describes the Eton College I recognize day-by-day, a school and community both confident and self-critical, in which over the best part of six centuries has evolved a philosophy of education that is liberal and wide-ranging, individual yet inclusive, and meritocratic.

To the casual eye, a visit to Eton can seem like a trip to a theme park. You might see boys and teachers crossing the streets dressed in what seems to be the funereal garb of the nineteenth-century gentleman. You might wander past buildings and monuments that resonate with history. You might hear snippets of conversation with alien words – 'half', 'beak' and 'div'. This is altogether another world, far removed from real life.

Yet visitors who spend a little more time in the school are struck by two things. First, that there is no portal through which one must pass to enter the school. It is true that the huge, sturdy wooden gates to School Yard present a barrier to the oldest part of the college, but the school itself is scattered around the public streets of the town, more like a small university than a school. Every building you see has some purpose as part of modern school life. Second, conversation with boys shows that they are keenly aware of the world of which they are a part. As one deeply sceptical professor of education put it, after an hour's stimulating debate with a group of seventeen-year-olds during which he had been impressed by their sharp intelligence, 'people out there don't know the half of what Eton is like'.

Eton is a place for young men who are expected to do something useful with their lives. Nearly six centuries of history are worn lightly – there is little teaching about Eton's past – yet this living tradition poses a question. If generations of boys who have passed through Eton have gone on to achieve remarkable things, why not you? Tradition is a prompt not a constraint. Add to this an expectation of excellence in each other, a belief in the virtue of being independent-minded and a sense of moral obligation to give something back to others, then that is a cocktail which gives young men the confidence to believe they can make a difference in the world.

For all the structures and management systems that are necessary to run a modern school effectively, Eton continues to be a place where the focus is on the young. It is a place where teenage boys flourish, a theatre of opportunity and possibility for a wide range of types and characters. There is no template Etonian. The school's philosophy is underpinned by two principles – that boys learn at least as much outside a schoolroom as in it, and that they learn at least as much from each other as from adults. Eton's particular genius has been, and continues to be, in creating an environment in which these things happen positively and well.

Adam Nicolson and Eric Anderson have not sought to write a comprehensive history. Instead they offer insight into the spirit of Eton; personal views certainly, but born of great experience, the one as a former King's Scholar, the other a distinguished Head Master and Provost. You are in good hands.

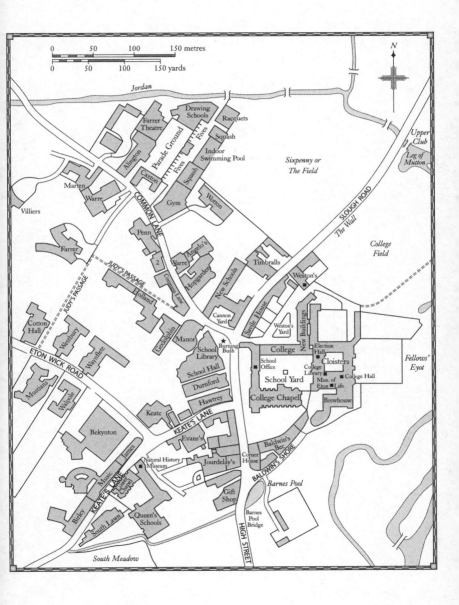

XIII

INTRODUCTION

THIS BOOK IS ABOUT ETON but is neither a history nor a guidebook. You could do worse than stroll round Eton with it in your hand to help you hear in the streets and yards, in the playing fields and gardens, the voices of a particularly articulate, complex, often rapidly-evolving community which has been here for nearly six centuries. But it is a book of glimpses, echoes, anecdotes and opinions, not a heavyweight account of what Eton is or has been. The idea is to give those unfamiliar with it as well as those who know it at least slightly some idea of what this most famous of schools is like.

The difficulty of describing the place is that there is not one Eton but many. Fifteenth century Eton and twenty-first century Eton are five hundred and seventy years apart. The school-lives of the boys, like life in the world at large, are not the same. Yet those lives are led on the same spot, in many of the same buildings and for the same purpose: preparing in youth for life in the great world outside. Modern Eton has grown from soil tilled for earlier Etons; there are echoes from the past for those who can hear them which still resonate today.

To understand Eton we need some feeling for those previous centuries, for the people who lived there then, the boys, masters, old boys, visitors, townspeople and traders, diarists, poets and novelists, some of them remarkable, most of them ordinary and not all of them admirable. So this little book begins with an informal history of the first five hundred years, told through the lives of Eton characters in different ages.

Three chapters follow which walk you round the ancient foundation buildings of the College and then through the school and the fields around it. The College, the historic core of Eton stemming from its rich and royal foundation in the fifteenth century, the grandest, oldest and most beautiful part, is where the treasures and the beginning of its story are both to be found. The word 'College' is also applied to the seventy King's Scholars and the building facing School Yard in which they live.

The streets to the west of the College, in which Etonians, both Collegers and Oppidans, spend most of their time, are not a beautiful collection of buildings – Anthony Powell calls them 'tenement-like structures, experiments in architectural insignificance' – but these are the realm of adolescent normality. This is where boy life happens. This is the school.

The rest of the town is really just the High Street towards the Thames, the old royal road from London to Windsor, now mostly closed to traffic and a kind of backwater in which antique shops and wine bars have proliferated like seaweed in a pool. It is a street which like many in the last twenty years has gone both upmarket and downhill. It is less important to the life of the school than the playing-fields and river.

The fifth chapter is about what Eton is like for those who teach or learn there. The final chapter attempts to describe some of the characteristics that distinguish modern Eton.

Every one of these chapters contains things which really belong in others, but that is part of the point. Eton is not a unitary, perfectly designed institution. Both geographically and historically, in its layout and its evolution, and in its culture and ethos, Eton has always shuffled from one condition to another. It might like to think that over five and a half centuries it has evolved steadily through the wisdom and energy of successive Provosts, Fellows and Head Masters, into an improved, bigger and better Eton, but it has never been like that. Between 1463 and 1476 it was in danger of being amalgamated with St George's Windsor. In eight disastrous years around 1770, the number of boys slumped from five hundred and twenty-two to two hundred and thirty. A hundred years later College was so dilapidated and fearsome a place that boys could not be found to take up King's Scholarships. Like the world outside, which in every generation it has reflected, Eton has had its ups and downs.

It is a school but it is also a town. Boys' Houses, masters' houses and classrooms lie jumbled together around its streets. It is both self-consciously stylish and pervasively scruffy. This is not a place run by the National Trust. It is stalked by self-delight, but can be a curiously anxious and overbusy place. In its ambitions, it has long been both idealistic and worldly. It has always been a place of display and performance, of battles of wits and fists, but also of loneliness and solitary musing. A great deal of love and delight have occurred here as well as personal unhappiness and fierce, political argument.

Nor is Eton hermetically sealed from the rest of the universe. It is more like a small city than a village, but one whose boundaries are not quite clear. The very fact that it sits next to the Thames and astraddle the road from Windsor to Westminster, two of the central arteries in English life, has been an important part of its story.

For centuries, Eton was less a single organization than a cluster of mutually dependent businesses: self-indulgent Fellows in the cloisters happily living off the rents from the farms which Henry VI had given them, Dames running rough-edged lodgings in the town, private tutors bemoaning their loneliness, cafés and inns, hucksters selling pies to the boys on the street, romantic dreamers alongside rakes and future Prime Ministers, even the odd individual master turning speculative builder in putting up new Houses for boys.

Some of that has gone. Eton has become neater, more tightly organized, more a single organism in the last hundred years, and in that way more like other schools. The violence of the eighteenth and early nineteenth centuries has gone, the extraordinary intensity of nineteenth and early twentieth-century friendships has diminished and the pervasive homosexuality, which was often frightening and horrible for small boys, seems virtually to have disappeared by about 1965.

But other things persist and the repeated element in Eton's story is a bubbling independence of spirit, a resistance to centralized authority, a mysterious kind of autonomy, occasionally finding its life in a crowd or at times a mob but just as often in intense friendships. 'The huge, formless school,' one of its veteran masters wrote in the 1970s, 'has taken five hundred years growing and its anti-authoritarian and oligarchic temper makes it difficult to administrate.' Provosts, Head Masters and Housemasters seem to bob on its surface, responding to it rather than governing it.

But that temper is also the source of Eton's vitality and

virtue. At any one time there are many Etons. The Eton experienced simultaneously by thirteen hundred boys and a hundred and sixty masters is not the same for each of them. There is no monopoly of authority, but instead a jostling ecology of different sources of power and value. College, individual Houses and to a lesser degree academic departments, as well as the theatre, the sports fields, the scores of societies and the drawing schools, all offer local hubs of loyalty and influence which have a more powerful impact on the boys than any Head Master ever could.

If there is a balance of power, it is too subtle for the naked eye. Hundreds of opportunities and demands are in a constant flux through the school. The boundaries between Head Master, housemasters, senior boys and junior boys are endlessly being defined, refined and exploited. The result is a sense of authority residing not at the top of the school but somehow disseminated throughout it. The energy comes from below and this 'low centre of gravity', as one housemaster has called it, means that Eton is constantly being updated in a dialogue between the generations. Even the most junior boy senses this. A full life is not given to an Etonian; he has to claim it from the start; and the energy, creativity, independence of mind and self-confidence to act which are necessary for a successful life at Eton all come from that demand.

No-one would think of designing a school like this. Its loose constitution has evolved over the centuries, in a classic version of the Burkean ideal, where the community of boys and masters has built towards the future like the web of life on a coral reef. Eton's tenor is the result of many, small, individual decisions, made over many centuries, not the product of a single, imposed vision.

As a result, it needs a certain kind of nerve to be Head Master of Eton, presiding as he does not over a set of conveniently arranged levers but the sort of diverse and localized arrangements which might have confronted a medieval king. Eton is not an authority structure; it is in an intriguing way a liberty structure, or at least an opportunity structure. Horace Walpole in the mid-eighteenth century called it a 'mimic republic', full of 'little intrigues, little schemes and policies'.

It still is a complicated place, impossible to pin down neatly. The inability to define it may well be its defining quality. As one master puts it: 'What Eton is, is not what people think it is.'

CHAPTER ONE

THE PAST

To BEGIN TO UNDERSTAND ETON you need some history. So let's begin with a few glimpses of the people who have lived here and given the place its peculiar character in successive eras.

It all starts with Henry VI's vision.

In 1440, the Lancastrian King was a shy and pious boy of nineteen, almost unable to speak to women, gentle and compassionate, neatly dressed, but no saint: he gambled and hunted and gave extravagant presents. When his great warrior father, the victor of Agincourt, died suddenly from dysentery aged thirty-five in 1422, this boy came to the throne as a less than one-year-old, a baby known as 'Henry of Windsor'. Surrounded by competing magnates throughout his childhood, Henry conceived an early desire for peace. He spent his entire childhood in the Thames valley, as much at home in his mother's language of French as in English, becoming a monkish adolescent, everything his warrior father was not. This Henry was the first English king never to lead an army against a foreign enemy and his lack of martial spirit forced him to surrender the wide swathes of France which his father had conquered.

His foundation of Eton in October 1440 was a turning away from the failures in France. It was an act of peace, dedicated to the Assumption of the Virgin Mary, the moment when Christ's pure mother was taken up into Heaven. Henry's purpose, as it says in the College statutes, was 'to transfer our temporal royal treasures into eternal treasures.' Eton was a denial of worldliness, a bookish, holy place, twinned with King's College in Cambridge founded a year later, the two colleges designed to be double adornments to England and its church. Through the 1440s, both King's and Eton grew in Henry's mind and by the end of the decade he was thinking of Eton as 'the lady mother and mistress of all other grammar schools.' Eton's purpose was to create a literate class of clerics whose character might mimic his own and who would become serviceable to both church and state. When all education was in the hands of the church it would not be surprising if the first loyalty of educated men was to church rather than state. Etonians, by contrast, would be good churchmen but also the King's men.

Much of what the young king set up was copied from Winchester, which had been founded sixty years earlier and which he visited several times. The first Master,

William Waynflete, came from there, as did the pattern of Eton's complement of seventy poor scholars, a Master, an Usher (or assistant master), a Provost, Vice-Provost, ten Fellows who were all priests, Chaplains, clerks, choirboys and 'thirteen poor infirm men'. The original Statutes were an edited version of Winchester's.

Henry VI gave Eton money (an initial grant of £1,000 a year for twenty years), church vestments, treasures (including a precious golden image of the Virgin, sitting under a vine laden with eighty bunches of pearls) and books. He made the foundation exempt from all taxes, shipped building stones from Kent, Yorkshire and France, granted it rent-providing lands, fishery rights in the Thames and gardens, houses and fields in Eton itself.

The King bought from the Pope powers for Eton to grant indulgences, for which pilgrims would pay handsomely to escape purgatory, and shipped in precious relics to attract pilgrims and their offerings. A piece of Mary's thumb, a lock of her hair, some of her milk, a finger-joint and part of the spine of John the Confessor, the 'Tablet of Bourbon' a kind of multiple relic which contained some of Christ's blood, another part of his mother, part of the True Cross and pieces of assorted 'other martyrs, confessors and virgins', all found their home here. From the beginning, Eton was to be a holy and scholarly place but not in any way poor or cut off from the world. In late medieval terms, the Founder was setting up a powerhouse.

After a chaotic reign, Henry VI was captured and imprisoned by his Yorkist enemies and finally in May 1471 found dead, it was said 'of pure displeasure and melancholy'. He had in fact been murdered, with a blow to the back of the skull. On the anniversary of his death, the Provosts of Eton and King's now lay lilies and roses on the spot where he is thought to have been killed as he knelt at prayer in his cell in the Tower.

Parliament declared all grants of the Lancastrian Kings null and void. Edward IV had Eton shut down, stripped of its lands and treasures, the foundation terminated as conclusively as its Founder, and the college made an annexe of Edward's own foundation of St George's in Windsor. Only through the intervention of Jane Shore, Edward's mistress – at least according to a tradition which began with Thomas More – was Eton saved, its lands and hopes partially restored.

Educationally, the place was a success from the start. At least a hundred and thirty Etonians educated here between 1440 and 1540 achieved enough prominence in life to appear in the modern *Dictionary of National Biography*, and in what feels like a strikingly modern variety: among the many clergymen, bishops, archbishops and college heads, you can find diplomats, logicians, humanist scholars, lawyers, composers, physicians, poets, a playwright, judges, grammarians, a Greek scholar, historians (one of them Edward Hall, whose *Union of the Noble and Illustre Famelies of Lancastre and York* was one of Shakespeare's sources), protestant and catholic martyrs, a printer, a map engraver, an antiquary, some MPs and a court jester, John Pace, who when Queen Elizabeth said, 'Come on, Pace: now we shall hear of our faults', uninhibitedly replied, 'I do not use to talk of that that all the town talks of' – enough, one might have thought, to have his head off.

Holy, serious, worldly, clever: that was the beginning.

EARLY SCHOOL LIFE

A handful of scholars as well as the first Head Master came from Winchester as seed corn for the new foundation. In addition to the seventy poor scholars, living in the College building in School Yard, other fee-paying boys called 'commensals', or 'eaters-with', and Oppidans – those who lived in the town, the *oppidum*, rather than the College – were taught alongside them in the schoolroom now called Lower School. From the start there were, as there still are, Collegers and Oppidans.

Each scholar had to swear that he would not be

a detractor, a whisperer, or one who abuses, or pro-
vokes hate, wrath, discords, envy, insults, quarrels or
disputes, or claims special or superior prerogatives of
nobility, family, knowledge, abilities or wealth.

These were the years in which medieval England broke
apart in vicious civil war, not least because of Henry vi's
political inadequacies. Comparisons were to be avoided
among the scholars 'especially between southerners,
northerners or hyperboreans' – no explicit mention of
Lancastrians and Yorkists, but the great divide hangs in the
air. No one was allowed to keep 'dogs for hunting, ferrets,
hawks or falcons, no monkey, bear, fox, stag, hind, doe or
badger or any other such unusual or rarely seen beasts
of prey which are not beneficial and may be injurious.'
There was to be no long hair or beards, no pointed shoes
or buttoned hoods, no swords 'unless they are away', no
long knives or other arms, and no 'red, white or green
hose,' no stone throwing, no 'jumping and wrestling and
other rough and disorderly games whatever.'

The suggestion of violence lurks behind every
prohibition.

But one can exaggerate the brutalities of the past.
Normality has a way of escaping the record in a way
that violence never does. Opening off Lower School
where the first scholars were taught is the Master's or

Head Master's Chambers. This was his study, with his bedchamber above it. Until 2006, there would have been little point in coming in here, but in that year, a College carpenter on routine maintenance discovered a coat of arms on the fireplace wall beneath the panelling. It turned out to be part of a rare early sixteenth-century **wall-painting**, most of it damaged beyond repair but with enough remaining to reveal a secular scene, a schoolroom, with a group of boys, a master with birch and book, and several Latin inscriptions. There are two coats of arms, one of Eton and one of Winchester. Most boys are sitting on a form; one is whipping a top with his pen and ink hanging at his girdle.

Here before your eyes is a picture of the schoolroom next door five hundred years ago. Suddenly the air of brutality and imposition dissipates. This is education as a tool of civility. From the records one or two incidents and remarks can be gathered around this crudely painted scene. First, on September 24, 1468, a boy called Hugh Chapman was freed from his status of villein at Piddlehinton in Dorset and allowed to become a scholar at Eton. His father may have been an Eton college servant. The freedman Hugh eventually took holy orders and in time became the Conduct or Chaplain at Eton. His brief life can stand as an emblem of the transition from the medieval to the modern world.

Next there is the description by Richard Cox, who was a master in the 1530s, of the life the boys were living:

> They come to schole at vj. of the clok in the mornyng.
>
> They say Deus misereatur, with a colecte; at ix they say De Profundis and go to brekefaste. Than a quarter of an howere cum ageyne, and tary [till] xj. and then to dyner; at v. to soper, afore an antheme and De profundis.

Some of the boys were living in lodgings in the town:

> When they go home ii and ii in order, a monitor to se that they do soe tyll they come at there hostise dore.
>
> When any dothe come new, the master doth inquire fro whens he comyth, what frendys he hathe, whether there be any plage.

Eton's piety and seriousness, bringing in boys from all over the kingdom and of many classes, its imposition of order in a disrupted world, are all there at the beginning.

The Master in the wall painting is probably William Horman, a Wykhamist who was headmaster of Eton and Winchester and finally Vice-Provost of Eton. If so, the book he is holding may be his *Vulgaria Puerorum*, published in 1519, a collection of sayings for the boys to translate into and out of Latin, some traditional but many taken from their lives at school. For instance:

> 'He hit me in the eye with a tenys ball'; 'A tenys player assayeth all the ioyntis of the body'; 'The apparel for this play cost me much money'; 'Gentyll mennys children shulde be most courtese and redy to do well', and 'It were as plesaunt and as good to teach an asse as hym.'

Alongside Erasmus and Colet he was a proponent of the 'new learning'. The scroll with a quotation from Quintilian which runs across the top of the painting has an astonishingly modern message: *Virtus preceptoris est ingeniorum notare discrimina*, roughly 'The virtue of a teacher is to heed the differences of (boys') abilities.' Exactly what the Head Master of Eton tries to do today: no straitjacket, but education as the drawing out of qualities.

SCHOLAR-PROVOSTS:
HENRY SAVILE AND HENRY WOTTON

There was a golden age between 1596 and 1635 when Henry Savile and Henry Wotton were Provosts.

Savile, even if almost entirely forgotten now, is a great figure, for his canniness and corruption, his ambition, his love of learning, his intensity of purpose, his wide-ranging internationalism, his making of Eton a place of world-standing. He is Henry Wotton's only rival as the most extraordinary man to have been Provost at Eton: scholar, courtier, politician, educationalist, mathematician and astronomer, 'an extraordinary handsome man,' according to John Aubrey the great seventeenth-century gossip, 'no lady having a finer complexion,' even if the full-length portrait of him painted after his death shows no library-pale scholar, but a powerful, manly, buccaneering figure in black robes and a lace ruff at home in the competitive world of Elizabethan and Jacobean England. He was a modernist, promoting Copernican cosmology when everyone else in England remained profoundly Ptolemaic, castigating the dons of Oxford (where he was Warden of Merton) as 'a constellation of ignorant, obstinate pedants', slewing his way into the affections of Elizabeth and many other European princes and scholars, the Queen's Tutor in Greek and Secretary of the

Latin Tongue. In 1596, even though he was not in holy orders as the statutes stipulated, he became Provost of Eton and set up a power-station of scholarship. He was 'a magazine of learning', running Merton and Eton as two parts of one estate: 'thus this skilful gardener had, at the same time, a nursery of young plants, and an orchard of grown trees, both flourishing under his careful inspection.'

His edition of the great church father St John Chrysostom, assisted by Hellenists shipped in from Oxford and Cambridge and made Fellows of Eton, certainly ranks as the greatest of all Etonian works of scholarship. There are witty, elegant and morally acerbic sermons in there which might, with advantage, be preached to some Etonian parents today. Take for example, the vision he describes of the Day of Judgement. The poor are calmly waiting for heaven. Their modest bags are packed and ready beside them, while the rich

in great perplexity, are wandering about, looking for a place to bury their gold, or someone they can leave it with.

The Development Department, which raises funds for Eton, would love to have it as an annual theme in Chapel on the Fourth of June.

Savile had been gathering Chrysostom manuscripts from all over the Mediterranean world since the 1580s and, once established at Eton, he set up a printing press on which the great work could be produced. The moulds for a most beautiful Greek type were acquired, probably from Frankfurt, and John Norton, royal printer in Greek, Latin and Hebrew, was hired for the team.

Savile became obsessed, fell ill and ignored his wife. When she complained that she would rather be a book, because then he might pay her more attention, he said that if she were, she would have to be an almanac, so he could change her every year. She threatened to burn the manuscripts. But the great edition of Chrysostom began to roll out, at the unconscionable cost of £8, 000 (at a time when the most expensive man-of-war in the Royal Navy cost £5, 000). It was a commercial disaster, tens of copies lying unsold for decades at a time, even when heavily discounted. The most beautiful copy, bound in crimson silk, is still to be found in Sansovino Library in Venice, sent there as a present by Savile himself.

Sir Henry Wotton was also a great scholar, a poet and, as the translator of Vitruvius, one of the first Englishmen to publish a book on architecture. Both Savile and Wotton as young men were involved in the English information-cum-spy networks, both were implicated with the proto-republican views of the wild earl of Essex, both were as much at home with politics as with a book and both were outstanding examples of progressive, early modern Englishmen. Savile founded the Chairs of Geometry and Astronomy at Oxford. Wotton was a diplomat, a student of optics, a collector of precious minerals and paintings by Titian and Bassano, a player of the viol da Gamba, an immoderate smoker, an early champion of classical architecture in England, a lover of the natural world, who 'would rather live five May months than forty Decembers' and a keen angler who fished from the College grounds with Izaac Walton. He called fishing 'his idle time not idly spent'.

After Oxford, where he had begun a lifelong friendship with John Donne, he spent his twenties abroad, making friendships among the intellectual and social elites in Germany, France and Italy. Sent by James I to Venice, he became famous for describing an ambassador as 'an honest man, sent to lie abroad for the good of his country', a witticism that nearly cost him his career. As Izaak Walton described him he was

> a man of a choice shape, tall of stature, and of a most persuasive behaviour, which was so mixed with sweet discourse and civilities, as gained him much love from all persons with whom he entered into an acquaintance.

He never had much money; his Kentish estate was small and as Walton wrote, 'For many years, like Sisyphus, [he] rolled the restless stone of a State employment, knowing experimentally that the great blessing of sweet content was not to be found in multitudes of men or business, and that a college was the fittest place to afford rest to both his body and mind.' The Provost's Lodge at Eton (Wotton had to buy the post with a £5, 000 bribe to the Duke of Buckingham) in which he lived his last years was 'a quiet harbour to a seafaring man after a tempestuous voyage'. Izaak Walton, in the *Compleat Angler*, said of his friend, 'I do easily believe that peace and patience, and a calm content, did cohabit in the cheerful heart of Sir Henry Wotton.'

The greatest monument for the two of them is Wotton's wonderful lyric, rejecting the fawning, power-creeping web of a court existence, in which both Savile and he had spent all their lives:

> How happie is he born or taught
>   That serveth not another's will,
> Whose armour is his honest thought,
>   And simple truth his highest skill;
>
> Whose passions not his masters are;
>   Whose soul is still prepar'd for death,

Untied unto the world with care
    Of princes' grace or vulgar breath;

This man is free from servile bands
    Of hope to rise or fear to fall,
Lord of himself, though not of lands,
    And having nothing, yet hath all.

It is included in the *Eton College Hymn Book*. On his death Wotton left every Fellow of Eton 'a plain Ring of Gold, enameled black, all save the verge, with this motto within, *Amor unit omnia*', an expression of hope, perhaps, more than experience.

His tombstone, next to Savile's is in the Ante-Chapel; on his portrait, from which he gazes quizzically at guests in the Provost's dining-room is inscribed the word 'Philosophemur', let us philosophize.

THOMAS GRAY, WILLIAM PARSONS AND CHARLES JAMES FOX

Eighteenth-century Eton is usually thought of as a rough and unforgiving place but it was here in 1727 that his mother sent the eleven-year-old Thomas Gray as a refuge from his abusive and violent father. Two of her brothers were masters here and they clearly encouraged her to think it a place in which a fragile boy could thrive. It worked. Gray formed lasting friendships with soul-mates Horace Walpole, son of the Prime Minister, who never liked going outside and who for the rest of his life could 'never see a *ballon* without thinking – shuddering – of a football'; Richard West, son of a Lord Chancellor of Ireland; and Thomas Ashton, a genius nicknamed 'Plato'. The four established what they called 'the Quadruple Alliance,' a joky reference to the alliance between England, Austria, the Netherlands and France against Spain, but for them describing a self-defensive little coterie of boys precious before their time. Jacob Bryant, a contemporary at Eton, wrote about Gray and Walpole in 1798 that

> they had few associates, and never engaged in any exercise, nor partook of any boyish amusement.

But by August 1742, even though Gray remembered his time at Eton as being surrounded by 'dirty boys playing at cricket', he had come to view it as a place of pre-lapsarian bliss, the first of many thousands of Romantic and Victorian ex-schoolboys who turned the Eton of their memories into the Eden of their dreams.

That August Gray was staying with his uncle at Stoke Poges (whose churchyard he immortalized in his *Elegy*), and from the summer-house there which overlooked a view of Eton and Windsor he wrote his famous, melancholy 'Ode on a Distant Prospect of Eton College'.

> Ah happy Hills, ah pleasing Shade,
>   Ah Fields belov'd in vain,
> Where once my careless Childhood stray'd,
>   A Stranger yet to Pain!
> I feel the Gales that from ye blow,
> A momentary Bliss bestow,
>   As waving fresh their gladsome Wing,
> My weary Soul they seem to soothe.
> And, redolent of Joy and Youth
>   To breathe a second Spring.

Here, the gloomy twenty-six year-old wrote, 'regardless of their doom, The little victims play.' It would be difficult to think of eight words less representative of the reality of Etonian experience: Etonians have rarely been victims of destiny, nor indifferent to the realities that await them. But their world-realism has often been allied to the atmosphere of the Gray poem – nostalgic-Arcadian, etiolated, refined.

There never has been an Eton type. Gray's near-contemporary William Parsons, for instance, could scarcely have had less in common with the aesthetes of the Quadruple Alliance. In the 1730s he embarked on his career of crime by stealing books, including Pope's *Homer*, from Mr Pote the Eton bookseller in the High Street. For one of his crimes he was said to have been 'whipped till the skin was flayed off his back and afterwards rubbed with pickle' – unbelievable even in the mid-eighteenth century – and after leaving Eton turned to a life of fraud and deception. He was finally condemned and transported to Maryland, but – and this is the Etonian turn – was so charming that he managed to persuade the captain of the ship taking him to America to allow him to dine at his table while on board. On arrival, the governor of the colony, Lord Fairfax, took him into his own house and treated him like the prodigal. Parsons stole £70 from the governor and made his way back to England, where he became a highwayman 'working the country between Turnham Green and Hounslow Heath' – the Eton to London road – and was finally hanged in February 1750.

In the next generation, Charles James Fox became the great Etonian. A brilliant boy, he lived in the House of a Dame Milward, who had him 'flogged constantly for playing at chuck [a version of pitch-and-toss] for guineas.' But he was 'infinitely engaging and clever' and as his friend Edmund Burke said, he was 'a man made to be loved.' He dined for England. He gambled, drank and swam in the river. One bargeman seeing the naked Fox clambering on to the bank after a swim was so struck by his 'excessive hairiness' that he said, 'Damn my eyes, Jack, but I believe there's Nebuchadnezzar just come up from grass.'

Friendships were the substance of his life at Eton. The party he would later lead in both houses of Parliament was essentially formed there, a lifelong 'cocoon of warmth and uncritical admiration,' as his biographer has described it. When they later gathered to oppose the government in Brooks's in St James's, most of the men around the table would have been at Eton with him. Fox shared the corridors in Dame Milward's with the 2nd Duke of Leinster, the Marquess of Cholmondeley, two Waldegrave brothers, the future Lord Walsingham, the second Earl of Ilchester, Viscount Galway, the second Marquess Townshend and his brother John. In the school at the same time were the future Lord Salisbury, the future Earl of Carlisle, the future Earl Fitzwilliam, the future Duke of Buccleuch and the future Duke of Northumberland. In this way, quite straightforwardly, Eton was the training ground for the English governing class. And the result was that for fifty years, or part thereof, in the eighteenth century and forty-nine in the nineteenth, an Etonian was Prime Minister. These figures are not a reflection of Eton's excellence. They merely show that for more than two centuries, whether Whigs or Tories were in the ascendant,

Great Britain was governed by an almost entirely closed elite.

Before we move on, one last Fox story needs to be told. In 1763, when he was fourteen, his massively indulgent father, Lord Holland, took him out of school on a trip to Paris. Charles was given a large amount of money with which he learned to gamble. Holland also arranged for his son to lose his virginity. So, according to his friend Carlisle, having 'had an arranged intrigue with a certain Mad^e de Quallens, of high fashion,' Fox came back to Eton

> attired in red-heeled shoes and Paris cut-velvet, adorned with a pigeon-wing hair style tinted with blue powder, and a newly acquired French accent… [which he] employd in declaiming against religion with a fashionable grace that wd. have charmed Voltaire himself. He gamed deep & was whipped with me [by Dr. Barnard] for stealing out of Church, to play at Tennis.

The surviving documents reveal the extraordinarily adult lives and arrangements of these Georgian boys. The Duke of Rutland's son, Lord George Manners, submitted the following in his bill for Eton expenses between Michaelmas 1739 to Lady Day 1740:

6 bottles port

14 bottles of Mountain [wine from Malaga]

Buckson breeches

Pair of boots

Pote the stationer (£2 18s 7d)

Powder, gloves, hair ribbon, pomatum, half a years' boot
cleaning (10 shillings)

Hay for the horse

Cambrick for ruffles

A set of silver knee, shoe and stock buckles

Horses to London

Can you imagine keeping such a figure under any kind of schoolboy lock and key?

DR KEATE, SHELLEY AND GLADSTONE

It fell to John Keate, the greatest of Eton's Head Masters, to bring the school at the height of its anarchy into some sort of control. Keate was the son of an Eton scholar and an Eton and King's scholar himself, a brilliant man who returned as an assistant master in 1797 aged twenty-four, was Lower Master five years later and in 1809 began his reign as headmaster which lasted twenty-five years.

One of his pupils, A.W. Kinglake, an adventurer and

historian, described Keate years later when trying to persuade a Cairo magician to summon a ghost from the past.

> He was little more (if more at all) than five feet in height, and was not very great in girth, but in this space was concentrated the pluck of ten battalions. He had a really noble voice, and this he could moderate with great skill, but he had also the power of quacking like an angry duck, and he almost always adopted this mode of communication in order to inspire respect. He was a capital scholar. You could not put him out of the ill humour which he thought to be fitting for a headmaster. His red shaggy eyebrows were so prominent, that he habitually used them as arms and hands for the purpose of pointing. The rest of his features were equally striking. He wore a fancy dress partly resembling the costume of Napoleon, and partly that of a widow woman.

His Napoleonic cocked hat, which he dashed to the ground at the moment of leaving office, can be seen in the Museum of Eton Life. Kinglake claimed that in every white-washed officers' mess or anywhere else 'in which English gentlemen are forced to kick their heels', you could find the head of Keate 'scratched or drawn with those various degrees of skill which one observes in the representation of saints.'

That is the man you must imagine in 1809 standing on the north steps up to College Chapel, attempting to call the roll of the entire school – in Eton terms to 'Call Absence'. Life had been entirely lax; Keate was here to impose a little discipline. As Monson remembered, he

> tightened the reins so suddenly that we were all in a state of rebellion in a week. One of the first alterations was to impose an absence after long church...The first evening this was attempted the whole school the moment Keate opened his mouth to call a name, set up a boo; that is, they made that sound which scarcely disturbs the lips, but at the same time, proceeding from 500 boys, prevented Keate from being heard, and he was two hours getting through the list.

In his time he suppressed several rebellions, earning a letter of support on one occasion from the great Duke of Wellington. One evening in 1810 he flogged eighty boys in a row, at the end of which the boys who had flocked to watch cheered and clapped him. In 1832, when he was almost sixty, he beat a hundred. According to a nineteenth-century historian of Eton,

'He chose to display a harsh dictatorial tone towards those under him, on the theory that a school should be managed by intimidation rather than by encouragement.' Whatever one might think of it now, one cannot doubt the courage it must have taken. He also knew when to turn a blind eye. Rowing was forbidden but everyone knew that it went on. On the Fourth of June, which was the day on which boys and distinguished guests took to the water, Keate kept away from the river but delayed calling Absence until well after the usual hour.

In the summer of 1815, after the defeat of Napoleon, Keate's ex-pupils entertained him to a tremendous dinner in Paris at which they teased him about the violence with which he had beaten them. Keate, while beaming at his victorious pupils, none older than thirty-five, 'took our joke in good part and in his turn told us that, if he had a regret, it was that he had not flogged us a good deal more.'

His sister-in-law's diaries give a glimpse of a more human headmaster than the memoirs of his boys. He was, she wrote early in his reign, 'sadly fagged by his great office'. Three volumes of Sir Walter Scott's *Woodstock*, now in College Library, bought in the year it came out, nicely bound and with Keate's bookplate, conjure up the pleasant picture of the great flogging Head Master resting from his labours by reading the latest best-seller in front of the fire.

Of his many famous pupils, two stand out: Shelley and Gladstone. Percy Bysshe Shelley is undoubtedly the greatest artist of any kind to have been a boy here. But he was exceptionally strange and Eton between 1804 and 1810, when he left for Oxford, was no place for such a boy. The mob of Etonians liked to pursue him. 'I have seen him,' one contemporary wrote many years later,

> surrounded, hooted, baited like a maddened bull, and at this distance of time I seem to hear ringing in my ears the cry which Shelley was wont to utter in his paroxysm of revengeful anger.
>
> In dark and miry winter evenings it was the practice to assemble under the cloisters previous to mounting to the Upper School. To surround 'Mad Shelley' and 'nail' him with a ball slimy with mud, was a favorite pastime; or his name would suddenly be sounded through the cloisters, in an instant to be taken up by another and another voice, until hundreds joined in the clamour, and the roof would echo and re-echo with 'Shelley! Shelley! Shelley!'

Shelley's strangeness was undeniable. He used to mutter lines from *Macbeth* and 'The Ancient Mariner' under his breath, which he added for effect 'to the natural peculiarity of his high sharp laughter at unexpected moments.' Seen in this light, his highly polarised personality, torn between the public and the private, the dominating and the victimized, appears as a heightened version of what almost every ambitious boy in this self-dramatising, highly competitive school has always experienced: a struggle to perform, a struggle to be yourself, a struggle to be liked, perhaps even a struggle to be feared. He was unfortunate in joining Eton a few weeks from the end of a school year, when friendships and alliances among his contemporaries were well-established but his Eton career seems to have ended happily enough. For the novel he wrote at school, *Zastrozzi,* he was paid the astonishing sum of £40 and he spent some of it on a leaving dinner for his friends who included many of the school's great swells. So Eton seems to have finished better for him than it began.

Gladstone loved Eton as a boy and remained devoted to it. When he came back for the last time in March 1891 to address the Literary Society on 'Artemis as revealed in Homer' – a speaking date arranged by the young and insufferable Curzon, who was still a boy at the school, and who had doorstepped Gladstone at a London tea-party –

the grand old man, who for some reason pronounced the poet's name as 'Oomy', spent the whole of dinner with the Head Master, Dr Warre, talking to the boys 'about the merits of sliding seats in the school boats.'

But when he began to address the Literary Society, his life-long love of Eton, its insistence on a classical education and everything that stood for, emerged in impassioned rhetoric. The novelist Maurice Baring was a boy in the audience, listening to something he would remember for the rest of his life. 'If the purposes of education,' Gladstone said, 'be to fit the human mind for the efficient performance of the greatest functions, the ancient culture, and, above all, the Greek culture, is by far the best and strongest, the most lasting, and the most elastic instrument that could possibly be applied to it.'

As he said these words his eyes flashed, he opened and raised his arms, and his body seemed to expand and grow tall. He seemed like the priest of culture speaking inspired words. His voice rolled out in a golden torrent, and as he said the words, 'the best and strongest, the most lasting, the most elastic,' they seemed to come to him with the certainty of happy inspiration and with the accent of the unpremeditated. With them, his voice reached its highest pitch of crescendo, and then, slightly dying down, melodiously sank into silence.

That world of high culture and Victorian assurance did not long outlive Gladstone or Victoria herself.

THE GREAT WAR AND AFTER

To understand what the First World War meant to Eton you need only look at the bronze plaques which line the colonnade in School Yard from one end to the other, recording the names of the eleven hundred and fifty-seven Etonians who died in combat. There had been eleven hundred and fifty boys on the school role in 1914: it was the loss of an entire school generation. In August 1914, a hundred and fifty boys left the school in a body, some of them only seventeen or even younger, anxious that they might be too late to join the action. Of the five thousand, seven hundred and seven Etonians who fought in the First World War, a quarter were killed (three hundred and twenty-four of them on the Ypres salient alone), a third decorated and a fifth wounded.

Thanks to the Macnaghten Library tucked away beneath the Provost's Lodge, no boy is unaware of that sombre time. The Library was given by Eugen Millington-Drake in memory of the fifty-three fellow-members of his House killed in the war and named after the House

Master, Hugh Macnaghten. Macnaghten drowned just after the war. He was deeply depressed by the loss of all the young men he had nurtured and it was probably suicide. Millington-Drake, a forceful diplomat, acquired every book he could find written in English, French or German by participants in the war and persuaded the vast majority of the authors to sign their books for him. To the original collection have been added trench-maps, postcards, sketchbooks, photographs, letters home and other memorabilia. There is an invitation to a Fourth of June dinner in the trenches at Gallipoli ('All those attending are requested to bring with them knife, fork, plate and cup') and a cavalry greatcoat, still uncleaned, hanging on the door.

The uneasy years between the wars were uneasy years at Eton too. The best-known characters of that time were typical of Eton only in their refusal to be typecast as public schoolboys. George Orwell held himself apart from Eton, Cyril Connolly wallowed in it. The only child of a Major Matthew Connolly of Bath, who was an expert on snails, shells, stamps and potted meats, Cyril was famously ugly, in a way, as Anthony Powell said, 'that women seemed to find irresistible.' He was known to Hubert Duggan, Curzon's stepson, as 'the tug who's been kicked in the face by a mule' and was said by David Cecil to be 'not nearly as nice as he looks' Despite that, and the lack of any sporting expertise, Connolly managed to get himself elected to Pop, 'because I was amusing', as the climax of a desperate, self-promoting Eton career. John Lehmann, living on the other side of the corridor in New Buildings, described Connolly as

> notorious amongst us, dangerous, shocking and exciting at the same time. The perfume of Sin that seemed to rise from [his room] was compounded in my imagination from the curling smoke of Turkish cigarettes, powerful liqueurs produced from secret hiding places, risqué discussion of *avant-garde* books that one could never imagine finding in College Library, and lurid stories of the forbidden world of cabarets, night-clubs and dancing-girls.

Connolly's brilliant description of his life as a Colleger in *Enemies of Promise*, published in 1938, focused on what he saw as the sterilisation of a literary sensibility by a 'culture of the lilies, rooted in the past, divorced from reality, and dependent on a dead foreign tongue.' All that this education offered in the end was the cult of the 'Splendid Failure':

> Were I to deduce any system from my feelings on leaving Eton, it might be called The Theory of

> Permanent Adolescence. It is the theory that the experiences undergone by boys at the great public schools, their glories and disappointments, are so intense as to dominate their lives and to arrest their development. From these it results that the greater part of the ruling class remains adolescent, school-minded, self-conscious, cowardly, sentimental, and in the last analysis homosexual.

When Eric Blair (later George Orwell) first saw this passage, he said he had to read it again, assuming he had missed the word 'not'. Surely Eton was *not* so intense, did *not* dominate after-lives and did *not* arrest the development of most people exposed to it? Connolly's theory was an absurdity which might perhaps have described the brilliant, lazy Connolly but nothing and no one else. 'Hunger, hardship, solitude, exile, war, prison, persecution, manual labour:' these, Orwell wrote, were 'hardly even words' to Connolly and his kind.

Connolly described Eric Blair, who was also in College, as

> tall, pale, with his flaccid cheeks, large spatulate fingers and supercilious voice ... one of those boys who seem born old.

But others (and photographs) describe a different Blair, with extraordinarily plump cheeks, 'large, rather fat face, with big jowls, a bit like a hamster,' and 'slightly protruding light china-blue eyes,' far from the austere, sunken-jawed George Orwell of his maturity. Orwell later rejected Eton for its snobbery. He was certainly poorer than most – his mother once had to borrow the money for Eric's train ticket back to school – and he seems to have adopted at Eton an almost underground way of life. Anthony Wagner, who was later Garter King of Arms but at school made tea and toast and ran errands for Blair as his 'fag', remembered Orwell as 'a kind and considerate fagmaster but he did not talk much.' He was a keen player of the Wall Game and wrote it up for the College record. Others scarcely remembered him being there with them. This was one side of College: a private reserve, almost an anti-Eton set within Eton, in which the clever adolescent boy finds his way almost alone. Near the end of his life, Orwell praised the school for its 'tolerant and civilized atmosphere which gives each boy a fair chance of developing his individuality.' That, expressed with extreme propriety, may reflect the reality of Orwell's Eton experience.

THE FIVE HUNDREDTH ANNIVERSARY

December 6th 1940 marked the five hundredth anniversary of the foundation of Eton. It was no time for
celebration. France had fallen, the Blitz was at its height
and the future looked ominous. It was decided to com-
memorate the anniversary at the chapel service on the
morning of the 6th, nothing else.

Two days before, on the evening of the 4th, two
bombs fell on Eton, one demolishing Savile House and
the other burying itself, unexploded, deep under the
Head Master's schoolroom in the south-west corner of
School Yard. Walter Hamilton, the Master-in-College
(later Head Master of Westminster) recalled seeing
the Provost of the day prodding the metal fin with
his umbrella and declaring, 'Fortunately, this one is a
dud.' It wasn't. It exploded the next day, destroying the
corner of the building and blowing the glass out of
the Chapel windows. The service took place on the
anniversary none the less. It was bitterly cold and
wind swept through the empty arches of the windows.
Boys were told to wear overcoats and scarves, but,
according to Walter Hamilton, that was the only
concession made. There was no reference whatsoever
during the service to the bomb or the state of the building.
As the Masters left the Chapel, Hamilton overheard one

saying to another: 'For the first time, I believe Hitler will not win this war.'

CHAPTER TWO

THE COLLEGE

THE ENTRANCE TO SCHOOL YARD is on the hornbeam-shaded gravel of the Long Walk under the archway beneath Upper School. That is the true and natural beginning to any exploration of Eton but visitors coming to look round are encouraged these days to come in through the churchyard to the south of the Chapel.

The **churchyard**, fenced with an iron railing, is the site of Eton's medieval church which was demolished once College Chapel was completed. One or two schoolboys are buried here, including one drowned skating, one burned to death with fireworks, and one, Edward Cochran, 'a fine young Gentleman and Heir to a great estate', stabbed in 1730 with a penknife in the heart while playing at marbles. The boy who killed him, called Dalton, although penitent and depressed, was found guilty of manslaughter at Buckingham Assizes.

On the right is the **Corner House**, a 1964 reconstruction of one of the oldest of Eton Oppidan houses (in use since at least 1596). This is where three Prime Ministers, George Canning, Gladstone (who loved it) and Lord Salisbury (who hated it) were all boys. To the left, just beyond the Chapel an oak door takes you on into the generous, lit expanses of School Yard. This asymmetric court – beautiful, dirty white, brick pink and grit grey – is the heart of Eton and always has been since its foundation in the mid-fifteenth century. It is unlike any Oxford or Cambridge equivalent, perhaps because the grass that once covered the spaces between the paths has long gone (in 1706). It was replaced by a packing of flints, which give a harder and more austere atmosphere. They were from time to time coated in gravel, but that too has long since washed away.

An attempt was made in 1990 to level off the yard, where during wet weather ducks were bathing in some of the hollows, and to relay the flints. A class of new boys were being taught about Eton's early days and learned that` the first pupils, homesick for Winchester, had scattered some earth from their old school on the yard as it was being laid out. It looked as if that earth might well be dispersed during the relaying of the flints; so they wrote to ask for some more. The Head Master of Winchester responded by coming over one evening. After Latin speeches from him and from a Colleger he presented some Wykehamical earth (in a plastic ice-cream box) and it was duly scattered on the relaid surface.

The rough-edged flints are uncomfortable to walk on,

like a floor of broken teeth, and you are better to stick to the flat cobbled paths which have been smoothed by the centuries. In the middle of the yard stands the railed-off statue of Henry VI, the Founder, put up here in 1719. In high-heeled pumps and flounced breeches, showing an elegant leg, he balances orb and sceptre like a glass of Chablis and a cheese-stick at a party. It may well be the strangest portrayal of a medieval king anywhere in England. The sculptor was Francis Bird, a favourite of Wren's, much involved at St Paul's in London, where the Provost of Eton, Henry Godolphin, was also Dean. Godolphin paid for this statue, but Horace Walpole, king of Etonian aesthetes, liked neither Bird nor it. 'The many public works by [Bird's] hand, which inspire nobody with a curiosity of knowing the artist, are not good testimonies in his favour,' Walpole said. As for this statue, it was 'a wretched performance.'

But the attractions of School Yard, as of Eton as a whole, are not in the detail of its ornaments but in its combination of parts. Here, each side of the yard is of a different date. The earliest, to the north, is the long brick range, built in the 1440s, which houses **College**, the rooms of the scholars of the Foundation and the lodging of the Master-in-College who looks after them. (The nineteenth-century oriel window on that side lights the Master-in-College's drawing room.) On its ground floor at the western end is the original schoolroom which since the 1690s has been called **Lower School**. To the east is the Tudor gateway, known as **Lupton's Tower**, which gives entrance to the **Cloisters**, Eton's inner sanctum, the zone of authority, quiet and carpets, where the Head Master, Provost, and the treasures of the **College Library** are all to be found. To the right of the Tower the gable and Victorian window of the 15th-century **College Hall** poke up above the battlements. Filling the whole of the southern side of the yard is the great stone, buttress-finned **Chapel**, partly a battered quarry of a building, partly the liner moored at the heart of Eton, eventually finished after a fashion about thirty years after the College range. And finally there is is **Upper School**, a large, 1690s brick schoolroom, raised on a Tuscan colonnade and built to accommodate the expanding numbers of the increasingly successful and aristocratic school.

Its scale, antiquity and solidity, indicate the seriousness of this place as an institution. This is not somewhere conceived for fun, or mere elegance or suavity or charm, or any other of the heralded Etonian virtues. This is a place intended to nurture and enhance a civilization.

On the opposite side from the Chapel Fourth Form Passage leads to the classroom known as **Lower School**. The extreme crudity of the bricks in the wall is noticeable, lumpen and irregular, made from clay dug just to the north, in 'le Slough' as the medieval accounts describe it, baked in kilns there and laid in extraordinarily fat and pudgy beds of mortar. Almost certainly, these walls were built in the early 1440s, the first elements of the King's foundation to rise above ground, by masons who were inexperienced in working with the new medium of brick. The walls are about four feet thick, dimensions more suitable to stone. The original plan was to build a cloister along this south-facing wall and the thin line of lead in the brickwork marks the place where the cloister roof was to come.

Lower School is one of the great Eton rooms, continuously in use as a classroom for more than five and a half centuries. The Head Master still teaches there and it is used by the seventy Collegers for music practice and for their evening assembly. It carries the marks of its long history. Its benches and desks, bored, grooved and channelled so that rivers of ink can be made to flow along their braided surfaces, all look medieval but are almost certainly early eighteenth-century. The paired columns which run the length of the room were put in and probably designed by the great Sir Henry Wotton, Provost 1624-39, both to support the floor above and as somewhere to hang pictures of the greatest Greeks and Romans.

All around you, the shutters are covered in the names

of the Eton Scholars elected to King's College Cambridge. The oldest names, from 1522, are on the westernmost window on the far side. By the early eighteenth century, they had spread all the way down the room to the panelling by the east door. The name of Sir Robert Walpole, Eton's and Britain's first Prime Minister, can be seen on the top right-hand shutter of the middle window on the south side.

Back in School Yard the huge grey-white bulk of the **Chapel** confronts you. Its rawness is part of its beauty; this north face is Eton's own sea-cliff. You could even take the advice of Cyril Connolly who wrote that he and his College friend Noel Blakiston 'sometimes walked across School Yard at night and lay on our backs looking up at the buttresses of the chapel for it was a discovery of mine that the height of the Gothic could be appreciated in that way'. It *is* one of the great discoveries: perpendicular architecture, with all its concern for height and purity, for the building as a soaring, sacred container, is best understood lying down. Henry VI would surely have sympathized.

Henry VI intended the building to be the great centrepiece of his foundation and his mind was exercised by it for many years. The king himself laid the foundation stone of the new chapel on the site of the high altar. He had a half-built version of the Chapel pulled down because he didn't like its 'to[o] grete curious werke' and 'besy moulding.' He also wanted it to be bigger.

The original church as planned would have been vast, one hundred yards long, thirty feet longer than King's College Chapel in Cambridge, and would have had a fan vault at least as magnificent. Only because of the huge weight of that roof, and the desire to have large parts of the chapel walls filled with glass, were the enormous buttresses necessary. But the chaos of the mid-fifteenth century meant that the building of the church stopped in 1460. It was resumed in about 1470, funded by one of the executors of Henry's will, William Waynflete, formerly Head Master and Provost of Eton, the founder of Magdalen College in Oxford, and by then Bishop of Winchester, the richest see in England. Waynflete's work continued until about 1479 when instead of a full-blown nave, a hundred and sixty-eight feet long, stretching west from the present building, he added a short, transverse ante-chapel and over all of it a cheaper, timber roof to keep the weather out. There is a statue of Waynflete on the outside of the Ante-Chapel looking up Keate's Lane past the traffic-lights.

As a result of this stuttering birth, the chapel does not achieve the grandeur Henry VI had in mind. It is just less than half the length he imagined, a magnificent stub of a building, carefully patched and restored since 1950, as if it were part of an abbey ruin. But even in its truncated state it has always played a central role in Etonian life. Memoir after memoir circles back to the Chapel as the emotional and ritual heart of Eton.

Eton is too big a school to assemble in any one building. Even the Chapel can hold only two-thirds of the school, as it did in 1983 to hear Solzhenitsyn (with a young David Cameron in the audience) thunderously denounce the evils of communism and the decadence of the West. So on rare great occasions like a Royal Visit, the arrival of a new Provost or the departure of a Head Master, School Yard is where the school assembles to hear speeches of welcome or farewell from the foot of the North Stairs, where Keate used to call School Absence.

The gap between the buttresses at the foot of the North Stairs is where the game of Eton Fives – a kind of squash which uses padded gloves instead of rackets – was invented. The usual entry to the Chapel today is the door under the Colonnade in the south-west corner of School Yard. Inside is the staircase which leads up to the **Ante-Chapel**, its floor thirteen feet above the yard outside as a way of escaping the chronic floods of the Thames Valley.

The Ante-Chapel is something of an Eton attic and needn't detain you long. There are plenty of memorials here to Etonian deaths in nineteenth-century imperial

The Royal College of the Blessed Mary of Eton near Windsor was founded by Henry VI in 1440 to educate seventy 'King's Scholars' and to honour the Assumption of the Virgin Mary. Half-way up Lupton's Tower , beyond the reach of the puritans' ladders, six angels tug a rather surprised Virgin Mary towards heaven.

The west end of the Chapel is decorated with vivid pictures of medieval life, a rich mixture of piety and violence, whitewashed over and forgotten for four hundred years.

The north face of the huge grey-white bulk of the Chapel, 'Eton's own sea-cliff', the truncated centrepiece of Henry VI's vision.

The eighteenth-century statue of the Founder in flounced breeches, under scudding clouds across the moon above Lupton's Tower.

A colleger practises his music in the original schoolroom, built in the 1440s and still in use. The pillars were designed by Henry Wotton in the seventeenth century and Robert Walpole's name is among hundreds carved on the shutters and panelling.

The recently-discovered wall painting of Eton boys in school in the 1520s, with its motto: 'Virtue in a teacher is heeding the differences in boys' abilities.'

A gallery of eighteenth-century leaving portraits (top left to bottom right):
Henry Hallam, Richard Wellesley, Charles Grey, Charles James Fox,
Henry Holland, John Waldegrave, William Young, William Cotton. 'Can you
imagine keeping such young men under any sort of schoolboy lock and key?'

The great Dr. Keate, Headmaster between 1809 and 1834, 'little more than five
feet in height, and not very great in girth, but in this space was concentrated the
pluck of ten battalions.' And two of his pupils, Shelley, Eton's greatest poet, and
Gladstone, for whom Eton remained all his life a place designed 'to fit the human
mind for the efficient performance of the greatest functions.'

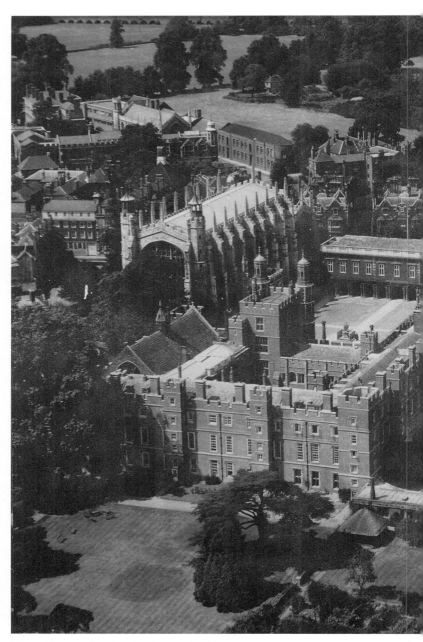

'More like a small university than a school.'

ABOVE: College Library 'exuding
scholarship and deep-carpeted thought.'

LEFT: A memorial plaque in the
Cloisters.

SACRED·TO·THE
MEMORY·OF
JACK
SCUDAMORE
KILLED·SEPTEMBER
25TH·1915·BEFORE
LOOS·AGED·19

'Effortless superiority.' Members of Pop between the Wars.

adventures (against the Indians, the Russians, the Zulus, the Afghans and the Boers). A painting by the Victorian GF Watts stands in the north-east corner, a day-dreaming Sir Galahad gazing at clouds. For decades, this was in the Chapel itself by the high altar but the story that the actress Ellen Terry (briefly Watts's wife) posed as Sir Galahad is sadly untrue.

On the west wall hangs a white ensign from the Battle of Jutland and a French flag captured in the Pas de Calais one night in 1915 by W. G. Fletcher, an Eton master and former King's Scholar. Fletcher crept across No Man's Land to the German trenches at Bois Grenier, where this flag was being flown 'boastingly' from a tree. Fletcher somehow hauled it down, crawled back to the British lines and brought it to England on leave. He was killed soon afterwards and his father, also a master here, gave the flag to the school in his memory. Everywhere are mementoes of Eton's great Victorian-Edwardian amalgam of romance and duty.

Side by side on the floor as you enter the Chapel itself are the tombs of the two great seventeenth century provosts of Eton, Sir Henry Savile and Sir Henry Wotton. Savile's bears his name, but Wotton's only a motto advising against controversy and the modest Latin words *Nomen alias quaere* – 'Seek his name elsewhere.'

Flanking the organ are two buttresses topped with a pair
of very early sixteenth-century statues, one of St Edmund,
holding an orb and two arrows, the other of St George.
St Edmund was an East Anglian king, who in 869 was
tied to a tree and shot full of arrows by the Viking Ivar
the Boneless (his real name apparently). Edmund became
the patron saint of England, at least until the fourteenth
century when, under the impulse of the chivalry-obsessed
Edward III, he was replaced with the great St George,
a Romano-Turkish warrior of uncertain origin, whose
virtue lay in his triumphs not his death. These two statues,
the oldest to have survived at Eton, were probably too
high for the iconoclasts of the sixteenth and seventeenth
centuries, but why they are there is something of a mystery.
St George was certainly a Yorkist hero, a favourite of the
macho 6 ft 4inch Edward IV; the saintly kingship of St
Edmund held a particular appeal for Henry VI, for whom
an illuminated verse biography of the martyr was written,
now in the British Library. It seems that these figures may
have been sculpted and produced by the same Italian-led
workshop which was fitting out Henry VII's Chapel in
Westminster Abbey in 1503-10. The twin presence here
of the Yorkists' dragon-slaying saint and the Lancastrians'
royal martyr, at the very entrance to the Eton chapel, may
perhaps be an act of symbolic reconciliation by Henry
VI, bringing together ideals which had been in violent

conflict forty years before. Henry VII was Henry VI's nephew. He poured a fortune into completing his uncle's King's College Chapel in Cambridge and these statues may be a small Tudor gesture to the sister foundation.

Under the organ is the entry to the **Chapel** itself. Here are row on row of seats in which you can contemplate Eton's greatest building. It has all the hallmarks of the perpendicular: linearity, purity, light, glass. As you enter, you feel that length stretching before you, a broad, long, handsome space pointing to the east. Curzon's friend Edward Lyttelton, who became Head Master and was a passionate cricketer, said he could never enter College Chapel without wondering whether it would take spin. All that is missing is the great fan vault which the Founder had intended and which the Tudor Henrys provided for King's in Cambridge. What you see above your head here now is a pre-cast concrete vault, suspended from invisible steel trusses, all inserted in 1959 when the earlier oak roof was found to be riddled with death-watch beetle. (The beetles had eaten so much of the timber than when a screwdriver was pushed into it, and holes made, sawdust poured out of them for five minutes at a time.) Brutally put, it is a muddle of a building in which the fifteenth, sixteenth, nineteenth and twentieth centuries are all at war. (The rather beautiful neo-classical seventeenth and eighteenth-century pews, screens and organs were removed by the Victorians in the 1840s and sold at Datchet railway station.)

But muddle is not what College Chapel feels like, particularly when in use. For years, services here seem to have been full of a kind of emotional seriousness, not exactly a religious feeling but something near to it. Because the pews are arranged facing each other across the width of the Chapel, one group of boys and masters spends the hour or so staring at the other, an arrangement which means that the school gathered in here makes for a powerfully social experience. Nothing was more beautiful, one Victorian thought, than a service in College Chapel, 'filled to the brim with gowned and surpliced boys, the hymns, the music from the fat-piped organ at the west end, the shaded candles glowing up on to the ranks of faces'. He rather spoiled the picture by adding: 'you could see Eton worshipping itself.'

In earlier centuries services were not always very reverent. Until the mid-nineteenth century, the junior member of Sixth Form provided almonds and raisins in Church, as it was called, for the rest of Sixth Form and for the nobility among the Oppidans who used to sit with them. One boy wrote to his mother in 1825: 'I should like you to see us all in Church some day, for it is rather a pleasing sight than otherwise, provided the boys do not pelt nut-shells and other kinds of missile weapons at each other.' That sort of behaviour was driven out by the Victorians and the twentieth-century doesn't seem to have revived it, although the young boys of the Choir School sometimes enlivened matters by tying together the shoe-laces of fellow Choirboys kneeling at prayer in the row in front of them.

The Choir School was closed down in 1968 and the funds diverted to music scholarships and to a Chapel Choir drawn from boys at Eton. The Founder, who provided for music in the Chapel, can hardly have foreseen that his boys would make recordings and broadcasts and take English church music to America, Japan and China.

Sunday services can be quite daunting. Anthony Powell wrote that 'rows of boys, fidgeting but silent, provoked, as always, an atmosphere of expectancy before the service began'. Visiting preachers have to be on their mettle, although the boys do give them at least two minutes to prove whether or not they are worth listening to. But even though it is a school chapel and the congregation under some compulsion to be there it still feels like a place where for five and a half centuries 'prayer has been valid', where there is a life of the spirit to set against the materialism of the modern world. The generality of Old Etonians may not be more religious than the rest of society but a great many read the lesson in their parish churches, a number of them work for charities at home and abroad and there is still a steady trickle of ordinands from Eton, many of them going to inner city parishes. One recent archbishop of York was at Eton, and so were the founder of Amnesty International and an initiator of the Alpha Course.

Boys are accustomed to moral questions. Divinity classes thrive on them and boys hear a homily at least two or three times a week in Chapel. That is the theory. Living in a Boys' House is the practical, a chance to learn from experience something about justice, tolerance, compromise and treating others as you hope to be treated.

So much for the life. What about the form and contents of the chapel itself? First, the **stained glass**. When the bomb went off in the corner of School Yard, according to Anthony Blunt's brother Wilfrid, who was the Drawing Master here, the Luftwaffe 'did us a service by shattering the Chapel's hideous Victorian glass. The art-loving beaks were quickly on the spot to collect and dispose of any discoverable fragment so as to preclude any attempt at restoration.' While the old lovers of dark and serious beauty wandered about looking for any surviving shard, Blunt and his friends stood on anything they could find.

Designing replacement glass was the source of one of Eton's great modern culture wars. For the huge **East Window**, the Provost and Fellows commissioned the Irish, Roman Catholic, modernist Evie Hone. Her

of Morris's insistence on the importance of the craftsmen themselves.

On the left-hand side of the altar is the grandest **tomb** at Eton. It belongs to the least significant Provost Eton ever had: Thomas Murray who was Provost for less than a year in 1622–3, squeezed between Savile and Wotton. He had been pensioned off here by James I (it is a royal appointment) after his job as tutor to the young Charles I had come to an end. It was erected by his widow who is believed to have declared herself willing to continue as Provost's wife should the next Provost be unmarried. It is a splendid piece of Jacobean funerary art, ornamented with skulls, hour-glasses and mattocks and a full-scale and very realistic skeleton at its base, from which some of the wooden ribs have been hacked away over the years by boys.

Pushed out from the chancel to the north, into spaces between the buttresses, are two small side chapels, the first, **Lupton's Chapel,** built by Provost Roger Lupton (1504–1535) about 1515, with a wonderful miniature Tudor vault, of the kind which might have roofed the great Chapel if there had been enough money. The Virgin Mary, to whom after all the College is dedicated, has found her way back here in the form of a little medieval statue presented by Provost Charteris. There is also plenty of evidence here of just how boring Chapel could be. In this little tucked-out-of-the-way chantry, the most junior boys had to sit listening to the service. They spent the time cutting their names into the stones of the east wall. Some of them are from the 1660s.

Next to Lupton's Chapel is the deep dark, guilt-drenched well of the **War Memorial Chapel,** sixteen feet by twelve but twenty feet high, designed in 1924, at the nadir of loathing for everything which the First World War had done to a generation. The cross in the north window fills the chapel with blood-red light and at the corners are four oak, deco-ish archangels, their wings brushing up against the roof.

On the wall on the other side of the nave there is a pieta, carved from oak in Westphalia about the very time of Eton's foundation, the gift of a well-wisher in 2008, and a simple stone plaque commemorating six Etonian martyrs of the Reformation, protestant and catholic. The Old Etonian former bishop of Coventry (where two of the martyrs had been burned at the stake) and Cardinal Cormac Murphy-O'Connor dedicated the plaque in 2003, speaking the words of the service together.

Out in the Chapel proper, just in from the north door, is the magnificent fifteenth-century brass lectern, nearly destroyed by the Puritans in 1651, when the College paid sixpence to have it whisked out of sight. At its corners are the emblems of the four Evangelists. The four small lions at its feet have been worn away by centuries of readers pushing at them with their feet to turn the desk around for the second lesson.

Now, though, something altogether more miraculous, the great **Wall Paintings** on both sides of the western end of the Chapel. In about 1479, Eton's second Provost William Waynflete installed a rood screen halfway up the present chapel. East of it was for the College, west of it for the ordinary people, as this Chapel was also the parish church.

Originally, the pictures were in two superimposed rows on each side: miracles of the Virgin on the north side and her protection of a mythical empress on the south side. But the sequence has been ravaged by time: whitewashed over in 1547 under Edward VI, revealed again under Mary Tudor, whitewashed over again under Elizabeth (by a barber paid 6s and 8d 'for wypinge oute the imagery worke upon the walles in the church'), panelled over in 1699, rediscovered and the top rows of saints and miracles largely erased by workmen in 1847, reconcealed under elaborate Gothic canopies for the stalls (the medieval images were not thought suitable for Victorian boys) and only re-exposed when the canopies were removed in 1923. They were at last painstakingly restored by Pauline Plummer over fourteen years in the 1960s and 70s.

What is left is a vivid picture of medieval life, sometimes

domestic, sometimes violent, sometimes exceptionally strange. It is best to find your own way through the maze of tights and codpieces, wimples and piety, and not be led by the hand. There is a red devil, Jews being converted, merchants selling their souls, an empress having visions, a boy thrown into an oven by his wicked father (at the west end on the south side in the upper row), murder, incest (at least proposed), mutilation, seduction, childbirth, child-killing, voyaging in a realistic clinker-built boat, a desert island, a devil in chains and a dragon in a girdle. In the stone-like tones of grey and lilac are tiny points of colour: bridles and saddlecloths, the jewellery around the Empress's neck. Almost at the east end of the north side, you can find St Margaret bursting out of the back end of a devil/dragon. He had swallowed her but couldn't keep her in once she had made the sign of the cross. At the west end of the south side, in the lower tier, is St Winifred, a Welsh woman who was decapitated by her lover when she told him she wanted to be a nun. Her head rolled downhill but was later miraculously re-attached to her body. A red line is painted around her neck where the lover's sword had chopped it off. She has recently become the patron saint of payroll clerks.

These wonderful and mysterious images of stiff, substantial but half-worldly figures are said by some experts to be the greatest wall paintings in northern

Europe. One standard work on English painting devotes
its entire first chapter to them. They are probably the work
of four different artists, probably from Flanders, probably
done in the 1480s. The counterpoint to these paintings
was the medieval choir singing the great anthem in the
Eton Choirbook, almost contemporary with them, called
Salve Regina, 'Hail to the Queen of Heaven'. Henry VI had
ordained that it should be sung to the parishioners every
day at dusk. The sixteen choristers and their instructor were
to process into the chapel and stand at the western end in
front of the golden pearl-bedecked statue of the Virgin.
(She wore a beautiful blue velvet coat and disappeared
at the Reformation.) The anthem was a setting of the
moment when Mary on her Assumption was welcomed
into heaven by the nine orders of angels (Seraphim and
Cherubim the trebles, Angels and Archangels the basses):

> Today the heavens welcomed the Blessed Virgin joy-
> fully, Angels rejoicing, Archangels jubilating, Thrones
> exalting, Dominations psalming, Principalities har-
> monizing, Powers lyring, Cherubim and Seraphim
> hymning and leading her to the supernal tribunal of
> the divine majesty.

The whole ensemble – architectural, visual, aural,
conceptual – was a reaching for eternity.

At the far side of School Yard **Lupton's Tower** gives access to the Cloisters beyond it. The Tower itself is the great Tudor building at Eton, put up by the Yorkshire Provost Roger Lupton in 1517, and carrying a Tudor coat of arms just above the clock face. Everything about the Tower is finer than the 1440s brick range to the north: better bricks, better laid, with stone quoins and stringcourses, and a big, elegant two-storey oriel window. The clock itself, now electrified, was only set up here in 1765 and at that time the two wooden bell-turrets were added, exceptionally sympathetic pieces of eighteenth-century antiquarianism. On the first floor are the arms of the Founder, supported by angels, and on the second the polychrome image of the Assumption of the Virgin. It has survived perhaps because too high for the reformers' ladders and perhaps because Provost Rous, as Cromwell's Speaker of the House of Commons, was able to curb the zeal of that second generation of iconoclasts.

It was from Lupton's Tower that a loudspeaker was hung on VE Day in 1945 from which the boys standing in School Yard heard Churchill announce victory in Europe. And this was the site of the night climbs performed by the explorer Ran Fiennes in the fifties. 'We did Lupton's via the front route, the north face, and we put a black flag on top. And we'd sit there drinking cherry brandy, by way of celebrating.' He has said he could never afterwards look at a building without thinking how he might climb it.

Entering the **Cloisters**, Eton changes gear and mood. Usually the visitor is restricted to the dark and always slightly dank wide stone corridor of the Cloisters themselves, surrounding a small patch of mown grass in which an unsatisfactory fountain spits and dribbles. Upstairs, one knows somehow, are beautiful drawing rooms and elegant furniture. Down here, though, is a certain boy-dominated bleakness. This dark stone passage is the route for Collegers from their rooms to their meals in College Hall.

Around the walls of the cloister are memorials to the death of Etonians in battle. All but a few relate to the First World War. One lists seven members of the Grenfell family who died in that and other conflicts. There is an unusual one for a young airman:

In memory of Henry Richard Deighton Simpson, an American boy of infinite daring, who returned from love of Eton to help England in November 1914 and was killed after almost two years of continuous service while testing a new machine, 20 December 1916.

The memorial for Colonel H. Jones, VC, by the steps

leading up to College Hall is perfectly round, to symbolize the parachutes of the regiment he died leading in the Falklands in 1982. The most recent individual tribute commemorates Lieut. Alexander David Tweedie, 'Died from injuries sustained in Iraq, Brave and True'. A memorial plaque to Eton's thirty-seven holders of the Victoria Cross and seven holders of the George Cross was unveiled by the Queen on 27 May 2010 to mark the hundred and fiftieth anniversary of the school's cadet force.

No-one has ever counted how many nineteenth and twentieth-century Etonians served in the forces, but Eton consistently provided more officers for the army than any other school. Twenty of them became Field Marshals. These days the cocktail of danger and excitement offered by the SAS seems to have particular appeal. But that is nothing new. Under the headline, ETON BOY STOPS A WAR, the *Daily Graphic* reported Sir Tom Bridges' account of a young officer who successfully ordered two armies to cease fire:

> I was in Tiflis in 1919... and I got a telegram from the Control Officer at Erivan, the capital of Armenia, saying war had broken out between Georgia and Armenia.
>
> The Central Officer was only a schoolboy, who had just come out from England, where he had been

in the cricket eleven at Eton and Sandhurst. I sent him a telegram to stop the war and delimit a neutral zone.

Riding a mule and accompanied by an interpreter and his servant bearing a Union Jack, he visited the opposing armies, and in the name of the British Empire ordered them to cease firing. He then ordered both armies back ten miles, summoned their chiefs, and delimited a zone about the size of Yorkshire, over which he made himself Governor. He enlisted police, appointed officials, and ran a first-class State for six months.

The pump opposite the steps up to College Hall once ran hard and perpetually cold even in midsummer but has long since gone dry. Up the worn ski-slope steps is **College Hall**. This was one of the earliest parts of King Henry's plan to be completed and was probably ready for use about 1450 but it has been heavily restored, once in 1720, by the classicising Thomas Rowland, and again rather more brutally in 1858. Unlike Winchester's hall, which breathes plain living and high thinking, it is difficult to think of College Hall as anything but a Victorian room, with its Victorian floor tiles, a big Victorian screen and gallery at the entrance and equally heavy panelling behind the high table with rather grandiose coats-of-arms everywhere.

It is an example of 'restoration' removing almost any sense of the past. One relic remains though. A square iron grid set at an angle in front of the oriel window was the book-rest from which the Vulgate or other improving literature could be read to the company.

The panelling on the side walls is from 1547 (restored 1858). One of the oldest panels has the following rudely-carved inscription:

> Queen Elizabetha ad nos gave OctoberX 2 loves in
> a mes 1596.

Henry Savile must have invited her. He had been her tutor in Greek and Mathematics and that was the year he became Provost. Queen Elizabeth II also lunched in College Hall, during the five hundred and fiftieth anniversary year of 1990. Extra loaves for the Collegers of that era were not apparently thought to be necessary.

For five hundred and fifty years Collegers have eaten in here. Besides boys' dinner in the middle of the day, Collegers have had supper in Hall and breakfast since 1919. Until the Victorian reforms their food, except on a few festivals, was always mutton, with bread and beer. Sheep would arrive from the College lands, and be pastured on

Fellows' Eyot till required. Bread and beer were baked and brewed here. Small boys would fetch the meals up the staircase from the College kitchen – a separate building, to minimise the chance of any fire in the kitchen spreading to the Hall.

The food at Eton has not always been of Michelin-star standard. An eighteenth-century Oppidan wrote home as follows:

My dear Mama,

I wright to tell you I am very retched, and my chilblains is worse agen. I have not made any progress and I do not think I shall. I am very sorry to be such expense to you, but I do not think this schule is very good...

The trousers have worn out at the knee, I think the tailor must have cheated you, the buttons have come off and they are loos at the back. I don't think the food is good but I should not mind if I was stronger. The peace of meet I sent you is off the beef we had on Sunday but on other days it is more stringey. There are black beetles in the kitchen and sometimes they cook them in the dinner which can't be wholesome when you are not strong. Dear mama I hope you and papa are well and don't mind my being uncomfortable because I don't think I

shall last long please send me some more money as
I owe 8d...

    Your loving but retched son
    T.H.

But it has not always been grim here. John Maynard
Keynes, on 15 December 1901, the day he was elected
to Pop and also heard he had won a scholarship in both
Maths and Classics to King's, hosted a College supper
here. That evening he wrote to his father:

> We had a most excellent dinner and I flatter myself
> that I managed the arrangements very satisfactorily.
> Your claret was especially appreciated as being
> extraordinarily good. We had soup, fish, pilaugh,
> turkeys, partridges, plum puddings, mince pies, paté
> de foie gras, dessert, coffee, with claret, moselle and
> champagne.

That sounds more like the fare reputedly enjoyed in the
rooms off the **Blue Corridor** above.

    A stone staircase at the northwest corner of the Cloisters
leads up to those precincts of power and authority. What
is now known as the Blue Corridor was once the open-
air gallery above the cloister but it was roofed in and
paneled in about 1760, as part of the Fellows' increasingly

comfortable provision for themselves. As Robert Birley once said, 'There was amazingly little to admire in the life of the eighteenth-century Fellows'. They annexed to themselves the huge increase that three hundred years had brought to the College revenues while leaving the scholars in the poverty and squalor of the middle ages.

With money sluicing through their apartments and kitchens, and their inconveniently distant, unvisited country livings being looked after by curates, the Fellows swam in gravy. In 1726–9, when the statutes were changed to allow them to get married, an extra floor was added and apartments enlarged, increasing the well-like gloom of the cloisters below. Although nineteenth-century reforms changed this whole system, there is still a sense in this corridor that it is a carpeted heaven above the stony hell below, an impression reinforced by the elegant, cerulean Eton blue (or is it actually green?) of the walls. Eton's use of the colour is as old as the school itself, stemming from a panel on the coat of arms granted by the Founder in 1440, which was to be 'pale azure with a flower of the French', the fleur-de-lis. That blue's lack of stridency makes it the Etonian colour par excellence. If a blue could be 'graceful, tolerant and sleepy', in Connolly's words, this is it.

The corridor is hung with likenesses of great Etonians in roughly chronological order. You can find prints of Wellington, Gladstone, Boyle and Gray, a drawing of

Macmillan by Stanley Spencer, Maynard Keynes in an oil of dubious quality, Shelley in an open-necked shirt, Head Master Keate in a bell-shaped gown, photographs of Douglas-Home, Birley and Chenevix-Trench, pencil drawings of Anthony Eden and Lord Carrington and caricatures of Thomas Arne and Henry Fielding. Leading off it are the (once exterior) doors into the Head Master's office, the Bursar's office, the Vice-Provost's Lodge, the Provost's Lodge and the Head Master's house.

The last of these was the scene of one of Eton's most amusing encounters with the great. In the 1930s, during the headmastership of Alington (whose daughter married Alec Douglas-Home), Jo Grimond, later leader of the Liberal Party, who was then President of the Eton Political Society, asked Gandhi down to Eton to talk. According to the playwright William Douglas Home

> Gandhi had that girlfriend of his, Miss Slade, with him. They came back to the headmaster's house where they were staying and Mr Gandhi went to bed because he said he was tired after his talk. And when Mrs Alington [the headmaster's wife] went to bed half an hour later, there on the mat outside Gandhi's door was Miss Slade lying under a blanket with a pillow. Mrs Alington said, 'Go to your room Miss Slade.' And Miss Slade said, 'But I've slept

outside the dear Mahatma's door for the last seven years, every night,' to which Mrs Alington replied, 'Not while I'm President of the Women's Institute you don't,' and made her get up and put her into her bedroom and locked the door.

But now to more public parts. At one end of the corridor is **Election Hall**. It was once the Library, for the Fellows not the boys, and the fragments of 1521 stained glass in its windows act as a catalogue to the books collected there. They lead the sixteenth-century reader to the shelves where, probably on chains, there were collections of books on Civil Law, Canon Law and Common Law, on Theology and Medicine, Logic, Grammar and Arithmetic. The elegant Tuscan screen was installed by the first married Provost, Thomas Smith (1547-1554), who used this hall as his dining room, and the long, narrow, highly polished table against the east wall (now thought to be a twentieth-century addition) was for shovel-board. Collegers ambitious to move on to Cambridge waited here to be examined during the annual July visit of the Provost of King's and his two 'Posers' in Election Chamber next door. Some have cut their names on window-sills. In this room now, on the first school day of each new academic year, the Provost swears in the new Collegers, who kneel in front of him one by one, as Latin words of the Founder are said over them. '*Sis bonus puer...civis honestus ac patriae utilis*: Be a good boy... and become an honest citizen, useful to your country.' It is a moment these boys remember for the rest of their lives.

The greatest treasure in the hall is the large, detailed painted aerial view of Venice, by Oduardo Fialetti, the obscure Venetian painter patronised by Wotton, who brought it back returning from his multiple embassies there. He hung it in College Hall in 1636 as a memorial to himself, 'a wonderful picture of a city that seems to float'.

The room is used today for lectures, small concerts and for 'Readings Over' conducted by the dons adjudicating Eton's great prizes: the Rosebery for history, the Queen's Prizes for modern languages and, most prestigious of all, the Newcastle for philosophy and theology. The Provost (for the room is theoretically still part of his Lodge) allows the boys' Political Society to use this room for meetings addressed by outside speakers. Harold Macmillan gave his last public speech here. Ken Livingstone spoke mesmerically as Mayor of London and Tony Blair, not yet Prime Minister, addressed the Society before spending the rest of the evening with the local party faithful in Slough.

A small flight of stairs leads to **Election Chamber**, which is within Lupton's Tower. This is Eton's boardroom, where the Provost and Fellows still hold their meetings and where, with all the small boys' papers laid out on the table, scholarships to Eton are decided each summer. Its seventeenth-century panels are hung with a great collection of early nineteenth-century leaving portraits. The portraits are more than mere decoration or sentiment: they are the residue of a whole set of relationships — personal, hierarchical, social, financial — which once defined Eton. It begins with money. At least from the early eighteenth century onwards, boys who were leaving were expected to give the Head Master a tip, £4 each at the beginning of the century, approaching £15 by the end of it (but double from noblemen.) This was part of a much wider tipping culture, entirely continuous with the worlds of Oxford and London to which the boys were now leaving. As yet, there was no school fee.

Robert Pierpont, about to depart in 1864, wrote to his father:

> I am afraid that you will be surprised at the amount of money I am going to ask for, but it can't be helped: leaving Eton is tremendously expensive.

Head Master	£10. 0. 0
Tutor	£15. 0. 0
House Butler	£ 1.0. 0
Boys' maid	£ 1.0. 0

2nd maid	10. 0
Groom	10. 0
Cook	£ 1.0. 0
Kitchen maid	1.0. 0
College Butler	1.0. 0
Boats	£ 2.0. 0
Musketry Bill about	£ 2. 0. 0
Musketry money	£ 2. 0. 0
Book for Mrs Young [She was his Dame]	10.0
Journey money	£ 3. 0. 0
Packing	10.0

Then there are I daresay things that I don't remember, and to leave Eton well, I should be glad if you would make this into about £44 or £45.

That figure is equal to about two years' wages for a gardener in the 1860s. To the later Victorians and in the twentieth century, this whole tipping system smacked of flunkeyism. There had long been a whiff of embarrassment.

Dr Hawtrey, the Head Master from 1834 to 1853, who was the essence of politeness, always affected to be blind to these donations. If it was at the end of the summer term, he would observe 'It's rather warm. I think I'll open the window,' and as he did so, the envelope was duly deposited upon the table.

When the next boy who was leaving was ushered in, the same routine was gone through, save that Hawtrey observed 'Don't you think it rather cold? I think I'd better shut the window.'

The famous Dr Keate, when receiving a leaving boy, with the window open and a breeze blowing, was seen to trap a £10 note under his foot where it had been swept on to the floor. Others, less frank, stuffed them in books where they have been discovered many decades later.

The leaving portrait may have emerged partly from that embarrassment, party from the eighteenth-century cultivation of friendship as an aspect of civility. It was a habit for Georgian cognoscenti to line their walls with images of their friends; friendship between a distinguished leaving Etonian and his Head Master might have seemed a natural extension of that wonderful habit. The idea of asking for a portrait came from Edward Barnard, headmaster from 1754 to 1765, and the first was painted in 1756.

The pictures gathered in this room are pupils of Dr Keate. An inscription high on the north wall records: 'Frances Keate, widow of John Keate, a fair, hardworking, learned man, who was for XXV years Head Master, gave these XXXIII portraits of Etonians to be kept in this room'. The only picture not a leaving portrait is that of Gladstone (who had been flogged by Keate once) painted in 1841 when the 32-year-old had become the 'rising hope of the stern and unbending Tories.'

Arthur Hallam is near Gladstone who loved his 'All-comprehensive tenderness, All-subtilising intellect.' Tennyson, for whom Hallam was 'My friend, the brother of my love', knew and loved him at Cambridge, a boy who 'seemed to tread the earth as a spirit from some better world.' Hallam's death at the age of twenty-two inspired Tennyson's *In Memoriam,* the poem which gave such comfort to Queen Victoria in her bereavement.

The leaving portrait was revived in the 1920s and again in 1980, but on the whole twentieth-century leaving Etonians gave each other and their masters nothing but photographs stuck to cards. These 'leavers' were said by Wilfrid Blunt to have been used in a game between bachelor masters in which the cards were divided, and trumps nominated, in the suits of 'the Beautiful, the Grand, the Clever and the Ugly.' The modern collection includes portraits of Timothy Gowers the Field Medallist in mathematics, Stephen Layton, Richard Farnes and Charles Siem (musicians), Bear Grylls on Everest, Matthew Pinsent the oarsman, Jacob Rees-Mogg, Boris Johnson and Princes William and Harry.

At the far end of the Blue Corridor is **College Library**, Eton's rare book library, which is open by appointment to visiting scholars, and is also used for teaching pupils at Eton and visiting groups from other schools.

A small College library had migrated to various spots through the first two hundred-odd years of the school's existence, was greatly enlarged by Savile, and finally settled here in the 1670s. In 1725 a new library was commissioned from Thomas Rowland, Clerk of Works at Windsor Castle. His design consists of three interlinking rooms, with a gallery on all sides. Elegant Regency furniture now stands within the beautiful, classical spaces, the architectural elements finished in unadorned pine, an Ionic order on the main floor, a Corinthian in the gallery. The room exudes scholarship and deep-carpeted thought. It is more like a gentleman's library than a school's and is certainly Eton's most beautiful room. The Turkey rugs are the original ones. By 2001 they were so shabby that they were about to be put on the tip until it was discovered that the Anatolian village from which they came still lived by weaving and repairing carpets. The Eton carpets kept the whole village in employment for a year.

Eton itself is about the same age as the printed book and from all five centuries of its existence the library has gathered treasures across the full range of European civilisation.

The best known book at Eton is the almost perfect copy of the Gutenberg Bible, presented in 1834 by

'Jack' Fuller, the eccentric Sussex ironmaster, sugar millionaire and patron of Turner, but the shelves are stuffed with treasures: the Eton Choir Book, written some time between 1490 and 1504, and containing a unique compendium of late medieval music; the earliest known surviving text of Ovid's *Heroides*; Alberti's treatise on architecture, with a few leaves in Alberti's own hand; early school books and early Bibles; Copernicus's earth-shaking little publication and Galileo's bigger one; illuminated manuscripts, including Mary Tudor's prayer-book; the great Sir Henry Wotton's letters; Dr Caius's annotated copy of Galen, and the original much-folded working manuscript of Thomas Gray's 'Elegy Written in a Country Churchyard'. The library is still collecting. Through the generosity of Nicholas Kessler, it has an incomparable collection of Chinese and Russian books, and thanks to Michael Meredith, manuscripts of Robert Graves's poems and Susan Hill's novels, relics of Browning and Elizabeth Barrett, hundreds of twentieth-century letters and an important collection of Gordon Craig.

College Library hasn't always been looked after with quite the meticulousness of the modern curators. In December 1859 the provost wrote to Thomas Bacheldor the College Registrar:

No one knows in what drawer the ancient catalogue is to be found. No one knows where any one of the documents mentioned in that Catalogue are severally placed. No one knows where those laid up during the last 200 years are to be found.

Whenever a drawer in the Library is opened, whether in the tables or below the bookcases, a heap of confused papers greatly injured by accumulated dust and occasionally by damp is discovered; there is in no one of these places the least order observable. There has been a very general observance of the System of Higgledy Piggledy which seems to have been – not for years, but – for centuries the rule with regard to papers and parchments.

At least nothing seems to have been thrown away. It was not until 1978 that the librarian discovered the last Will of Henry v, and recently a scholar unearthed the first secular contemporary reference to Robin Hood. It is not at all complimentary.

Virtually all of pre-modern Eton has now been described except for **Upper School** above the entrance to School Yard and approached by the staircase leading to the Chapel. In Keate's time, when a boy was promoted from Lower to Upper School he had to undergo the ceremony of 'booking' on these stairs, a gauntlet of Upper School boys trying to hit him on the head with their books. It is the last of the great inherited Eton spaces, a schoolroom built in the 1690s to accommodate the growing numbers. Several classes were taught at once, each of the four or five assistant masters in the raised desks on either side, the Head Master's desk at the far end. By the time of Keate a room designed for elegance had become the cockpit of disruption. Up to two hundred boys were taught here at the same time. Sometimes, at moments of total breakdown, the only possible response was violent suppression of free spirits. A previous Head Master had been driven out of his schoolroom in 1782, and Keate himself was once pelted with so many eggs that he had to go home to change. On arrival in Upper School, he usually trimmed the wicks of the candles with a snuffer. Boys liked to put gunpowder in the snuffers so that the first candle went out with an explosion. They nailed up the doors into his desk. He vaulted over the barrier. Shelley was suspected of putting a bulldog in there. Gladstone was flogged by him but only once, in a regime the Prime Minister would later and probably correctly call 'terror without cruelty.' One day, Keate was just missed by a stone which, though thrown at a chandelier, almost killed him. At the end of one lesson, he is said to have found himself stuck to his seat with a lump of cobbler's wax which a boy had put there beforehand.

The busts of famous Etonians line the walls. They date from 1840 when the colonial administrator Lord Wellesley presented one of himself, soon followed by his younger brother the Duke of Wellington. The four over the south door are of George III, William IV, to which the boys subscribed £200, Queen Victoria and the Prince Consort. Waldo Story's bust of Shelley (to which Rosebery, Swinburne and Robert Bridges all subscribed), was rejected by the Provost when it was first offered, because he would not have Upper School defiled by the bust of an atheist. They are accompanied by five more prime ministers, Lords Grenville, Grey, Walpole, Chatham and (to the astonishment of American visitors who are not brought up to admire him) Lord North; a great Etonian oppositionist, Charles James Fox; three classical scholars, Pearson, Hammond, Porson; a Lord Chief Justice, Denman; a single writer, Henry Fielding; and an admiral, Lord Howe. Curzon, with three of his friends, once played tennis in here, undetected for an hour, 'while tennis balls cannoned off the heads of Chatham and Canning and other giants of former days.' Every inch of the panelling is covered in boys' names, often in family groups, some carved professionally and some by boys themselves. You can find Shelley and Gladstone and, on one of the doors,

Birendra of Nepal and his son, Dipendra, who murdered
him. Just outside on the landing are Prince William and
Prince Harry.

Through the doors at the northern end of Upper School
is the **Head Master's Schoolroom**, previously one
of the locations for the school library, now decorated
with plaster casts of the Elgin Marbles. The author and
publisher Nigel Nicolson describes a lesson here with the
great Robert Birley:

> He taught the Headmaster's division classical history,
> and his classes were always those most looked forward
> to. He would say, 'Today we are going to talk about
> one of the most extraordinary events in history –
> the Sicilian campaign', and would then describe the
> ships, the armour, the politics, the battle, the danger,
> the glory, all with such emotion and sense of fun (he
> adored speaking of war, oddly enough) that we felt
> we were actually in Sicily in 420 BC, rowing in the
> galleys, slaving in the mines, speaking in the Assembly.
> Robert's very shyness made us adore him. It was as
> if he were another boy, not a master. Discipline was
> something unknown and unnecessary with him. He
> treated us like undergraduates. For the first time we
> saw what fun it was to be adult, and how it was

possible for a shy man to be a dominating man, and
that intelligence was not arid.

This was also the scene of the Head Master's floggings.
Boys took it nobly. From the journal of Charles Golightly,
aged fifteen in 1822:

> After supper learn my Homer. Friday morning
> unable to say my 70 lines of Homer.
>   Am flogged at 12 o'clock, do not change counte-
> nance; feel composed in my mind and serene.

Even in today's more humane Eton, this room is
associated with punishment. Each day before lunch the
Head Master sits in judgement here on boys who have
broken a school rule in the previous twenty-four hours.
Their Housemasters put them on the list of malefactors
(in Eton parlance 'in the Bill'), they are summoned by
two praepostors, the rather elevated title of the prefects
in charge of the Head Master's punishment schedule.
Most recent Head Masters think as they take up office
that they will pass this daily chore to an underling but,
so far, none has. The opportunity it gives them to keep
a finger on the pulse of the school and to become
acquainted with some of its lively characters has proved
too valuable.

This was the room almost entirely destroyed by the bomb which blew out the Chapel glass in December 1940. Before it exploded there was time to remove Keate's table, the bust of the Duke of Newcastle and the doors, and to photograph the names of Sixth Form and Newcastle Scholarship winners carved on the panelling so that the room could be accurately restored after the war. You can see which fragments of the panelling survived and which had to be renewed.

The names on the honours' board record the winners and runners-up in the Newcastle Scholarship from 1829 to the present day. This is competed for annually by the cleverest boys in the school and marked by a visiting examiner from one of the universities. You can find the names of Quintin Hogg, Douglas Hurd and the present Provost, William Waldegrave, up there in gold.

The names carved into the panelling are those of Sixth Form, in other words of the cleverest King's Scholars and the cleverest Oppidans in the top year. You can find quite a few famous names here. To the left of the door there is a constellation of stars. Sixth Form in 1947 and 48 included Robert Armstrong, who became Cabinet Secretary, Tony Lloyd (Appeal Court judge), John Barton (Artistic Director of the Royal Shakespeare Theatre), Julian Slade who wrote musicals, Robin Leigh-Pemberton (Governor of the bank of England) and Douglas Hurd (the Foreign Secretary).

CHAPTER THREE

THE SCHOOL

IT USED TO BE A great Eton crime to sit on the long, low stretch of wall outside Upper School, separating the **Long Walk** from the road. This was Pop Wall. For an ordinary boy to sit here was an act of Etonian lese-majesty. Only members of Pop, the group of about twenty self-elected senior boys, were allowed to sit here, just as they were the only Etonians allowed to walk arm in arm, or along the High Street on the east side, to have their umbrellas tightly rolled, the collars of their overcoats turned *down*, blobs of sealing wax dropped on to the brims of their top hats, black braid sewn on their tail coats, coloured silk made into their waistcoats and grey, sponge-bag cloth used for their trousers. The point? None of it meant anything, unless you subscribed to the code, but if you did, as almost without exception Etonians did, it became indistinguishable from everything that mattered.

Pop started in 1811, as the Eton Society, in Mrs Hatton's sock-shop or *popina,* a social club—cum-debating society whose members were called the Literati. They held a weekly debate and had a weekly breakfast. The Society was at first astonishingly high-minded and has gone downhill since first conceived. For a flavour of its early tone, this is a letter written by the much-beloved Arthur Hallam in March 1827 to his friend the hyper-Tory William Windham Farr who had already gone up to Cambridge. To avoid overt political wrangling, the rules of the Society did not allow them to debate any issue which had been live in the previous fifty years.

> Our friend Gladstone seems to find a congenial atmosphere in the 6th. form, & is dignified towards lower boys; a species of rigor which is nowadays most rare, as the inferiors are more presuming, & the superiors more lax than I ever reme[mber.]

They had had a 'spirited session' debating such topics as:

> 'Augustus, is he to be admired?' Carried for the Noes;
> 'Sir R. Walpole, did he deserve well of his country?' Carried for the Ayes, and '*Mohammed,* is he to be admired?' Carried for the Noes.

Such self-conscious and wide-ranging intellectuality was perhaps unlikely to survive and Pop slewed into something altogether more powerful and less refined, becoming by the middle of the nineteenth century a self-perpetuating gang of bloods and swells. Simply put, the natural leaders of boys – the strong, the sporting, the handsome, the charming – took it over as the vehicle of their dominance of what Horace Walpole called their 'mimic republic'. After a visit to Eton, Gladstone was so distressed to find a picture of a Derby winner above the mantelpiece of the Pop Room, that he was moved to write to his successor as Prime Minister, Lord Rosebery, suggesting that he should address the authorities at Eton on the subject. Rosebery felt less strongly than his great predecessor: the Derby winner was one of his horses.

By the late twentieth century, Pop had lost a great deal of its dignity. Christopher Hollis, the Conservative MP and historian of Eton in the 1960s, considered it 'a bad institution, for it encouraged shameless and degrading toadying by those who wanted to get in to those who were already in.' Perhaps it always had.

Finally, in 1985, the gods' wings were clipped. The cleaning lady working in Pop Room applied to the authorities, in all innocence, for more and larger ashtrays, as those already in use, she explained helpfully, were always overflowing. Selection of members of Pop is now as much the responsibility of a committee of young masters and the recommendation of Housemasters as of the boys themselves. Pop has become almost indistinguishable from the body of prefects in any school. Its own precious records, which at one point were being abused, have been removed for safe-keeping to College Library and

Pop Room is now a rather dusty ghost of its former self although the tradition of vulgarly colourful waistcoats still survives.

So have no fear. Pop has shrunk from its glory days and you can enjoy sitting on the Wall like 1789 citizens lounging on the settees of the Tuileries.

This gravelled walk is the boundary between the old foundation of the College and the school that clusters at its gate. George III used to chat here with boys on his way back from hunting. Here from time to time Etonians have cheered sovereigns as they rode past, to or from Windsor. And here they used to assemble to applaud the oarsmen who had won races on the river. Eric Parker, in July 1914 nostalgically remembered Eton thirty years before, when

> the school stood by the wall in front of the chapel and Upper School. Most of Pop gathered in the road; a few, with canes, walked up and down to keep the line. The winner of the race was hoisted, the second, the third: each in turn was seized, and threw his arms round the necks of two; each was grasped by the trouser-leg by two more, and run from the Christopher Yard to Keate's Lane and back again, Pop running beside and cheering as they ran.

This Long Walk was also, until Keate threw them out, the shared pitch for 'sock-cads', street vendors of food – 'cad' was a universal eighteenth-century elite term for anyone from the lower classes, 'sock' more mysteriously the Eton word for sweets or a snack.

At this point the realm of royal establishment gives way to the world of the entrepreneurial spirit. As Peter Lawrence, the Eton master and historian, has written:

> For centuries everything not strictly college was private enterprise. The Head Master paid the assistant masters. Oppidan parents paid Tutors and mathematical Masters direct, and board-and-lodging was a matter for individual negotiation. All games, musketry, gym, clerks, watchmen, cleaners, lighting etc. were paid for separately. Not till 1920 was an inclusive school fee introduced. Even then housemasters continued to own the fabric and the furnishings of the buildings in which the boys were housed.

In Victorian and Edwardian Eton, it was the masters who started and financed the laundry, the gasworks, the chain of school shops, the boathouses, the outlying football fields, as well as the fives, squash and rackets courts. And although Victorian Housemasters, who in effect ran their own businesss, were exceptionally well rewarded, and although it was said that no school in Victorian England charged more for so little, the boys and their parents had high expectations. In 1861, the assistant master C.C. James, speaking from experience, complained that 'A man could not set up a tutor's house at Eton without very considerable outlay, perhaps from £3, 000 to £6, 000. Furniture was a very considerable item. The boys would turn up their noses if you did not give them silver forks and spoons.'

As you look across the road from the Long Walk, you will see, first, two rather bleak Boys' Houses, **Hawtrey** and **Durnford**, hideous products of the boom in Eton boarding which came with the railways in the 1840s. Few buildings could look less happy or charming, but they are only of this form because they are designed to accommodate one of the great features of Eton: a room for every boy, however small. A building consisting of fifty bedroom-studies and little else, with a house for a master and his family tacked on the front, is not a good recipe for architectural elegance. These buildings tend to look like gents' houses which have sprouted a barracks out the back. And conditions in the Houses were far from luxurious. When Shane Leslie's hero in his 1899 novel *The Oppidan* arrived at his House for the first time, he

found himself crouching in a low room, whose ceiling must have suffered in a geological catastrophe. The room was no doubt commodious, when not entirely occupied with a table, a bureau, a Windsor chair, a can, a footbath, and a curious cupboard which opened in order to vomit a bed. A thick smoke was the only indication that a fire had been previously lit. Mrs Sowerby [the dame who 'weighed fifteen stone and resembled a duchess dressed as a governess'] opened the window and Peter looked round at his furniture. The bureau was the most curious. It was a carpenter's chimaera of threefold construction. Its head was a bookcase, its belly was a writing desk and its tail was a chest of drawers. Under the table was an awkward box upholstered in drab purple, which Mrs Sowerby addressed as an ottoman. It proved to be the local hybrid between a sofa and a packing case, rather neatly combining the deficiencies of both. 'Any cigarettes or catapults?' she asked, with a ferrety gleam in her wax face.

A few yards down **Keate's Lane** on the left hand side is a mark in the wall which shows where the west end of the chapel would have been if Henry VI's intentions had not been destroyed by civil war. On this side is the Boys' House known as **Evans's** and opposite is **Ballard's**, now the house of the Precentor, the master in charge of music at Eton.

With its arched gateways and its air of a converted inn, Evans's remains one of the few Houses at Eton which retains some of the atmosphere of earlier centuries. This was the building known in the eighteenth century as 'the House of Lords.' Half close your eyes and you can imagine a pair of aristocratic parents visiting in the 1750s, summing it up as a place for their heir and hope. There is no need to be too romantic about this: a 1952 report on Evans's described one room which 'contained the boiler, the gas rings for cooking and the racks holding the football boots. With no external ventilation, it is the place boys like to linger in winter'. This is also where the boys used to take their occasional baths. Brian Johnson, the cricket commentator, who boarded in the now-disappeared Coleridge House in Keate's Lane in the 1930s remembered

> We had forty to forty-five boys, and one tin bath which you put in front of the fire. You had one bath a week. I remember the housemaster would come round and say, 'What are you doing little boy?' I said 'Having a bath,' and he said 'Lucky dog.'

It won't have been any better in the eighteenth century.

Four generations of the Evans family worked at Eton, from the eighteenth to the twentieth century, teaching drawing in the studio-schoolroom across the road from the House. In 1837 the drawing-master, William Evans, was persuaded to buy out the dame who had the dilapidated building opposite his studio and convert it at his own expense into a House. He fed and housed his boys so well that one dame called out whenever he passed her window, 'Oh William Evans, William Evans, you are ruining us all!' At his death in 1877 his daughter Jane, the last of the Dames, succeeded him; and remained there until 1906. From that time on all Boys' Houses were run by men until 2007 when Dr Jane Sillery became Master-in-College. The title of 'Dame' is now reserved for Eton's powerful house matrons.

The small pair of schoolrooms half way up Keate's Lane, once William Evans's studio, have their own florid history. The building was an eighteenth-century wash house, converted at the end of the century into a pupil room where Lord Wellesley and probably his brother the Duke of Wellington were both taught. But with the Evanses, who were art teachers, it became the Drawing Schools. 'The old studio in Keate's Lane,' as Anthony Powell remembered it,

> across which trailed a purple wistaria, consisted of two moderately sized sky-lighted rooms opening into each other. These rooms were always in a state of comfortable disorder; piled up with pictures, plaster casts, oddments of silver, china or glass, suitable for forming 'still life' compositions.

Over this 'nook of the Latin Quarter' Sidney Evans, the last of the dynasty, presided as a warm, avuncular, near-Bohemian presence removed from the ya-ya of sporting, philistine Eton beyond its windows.

It became the stage set and headquarters late in 1921 of The Eton Society of Arts, the most extreme flowering of Eton's latent dandyism. Anthony Powell, the aesthete Harold Acton, who hung a Whistler nocturne on the walls of his room – 'an oasis in the desert of hunting prints' – the travel writer Robert Byron and Henry Yorke, all of them dandies, poseurs and aesthetes, were members. Their king and leader (although Powell despised him) was the anglicized American Brian Christian de Claibourne Howard (a Euro-aristo name entirely invented by his parents who were called Gassaway.)

This art-room was the Society's salon and the attitude of the school towards it, according to Robert Byron, 'resembled that of someone discovering the first symptoms of leprosy in his mother.'

Howard alternated Virginian jazz with the 'Liebestod' from *Tristan* on his gramophone, wrote vogue-ish, sub-Eliot poetry, remarkable for a fifteen-year-old, and had it published by the Sitwells. His teachers hated him ('It has seldom been my lot, in many years of work amongst boys, to come upon one so entirely self-centred and egotistical') but Howard was authentically of the avant-garde, introducing in his extraordinary 1922 ephemeral

Eton Candle, largely written by members of the Eton Society of Arts, the names of Stravinksy, Ravel, Cézanne, Epstein, Rodin and Rimbaud in a school still entranced by Housman, Elgar and Ruskin.

The next building on the right side of the road is the elegant, red brick **Keate House** (the central block 1788) which was indeed where Keate lived when headmaster and from which he walked to work every day up the lane. This was in the 1850s the house where Algernon Swinburne, Eton's greatest poet after Shelley, was a boy. Like Shelley he had trouble from some of his contemporaries: 'If you ever see him, kick him, or if he is too far off, throw a stone' was the advice of a senior boy.

This is also the house in which David Fraser, the twentieth-century general and novelist, boarded in the late 1930s. Usually, twentieth century memoirists disparage Eton but Fraser loved it and no part of it more than his Housemaster J. D. Upcott:

> Upcott was a man of the world, openly derisory of some of the pettier habits of schoolmasters and frankly mocking of some of his colleagues. He taught us to laugh at a lot of life, and especially at ourselves.
>
> He was a kind man; but he never encouraged a boy to take set-backs tragically or make much of physical pain.
>
> His friendship was always extended on equal and

uncondescending terms. He relished the English language, easily communicated enthusiasm, and liked an argument, which he would conduct fairly but vigorously, using a good deal of personal abuse, which he expected to be reciprocated. He would say after some verbal exchange of shots with me on his evening tour of the house to say goodnight, 'What's the use of arguing with you, you're a reactionary and obstinate little Scotsman,' and I would retort, 'And you're a narrow-minded Devonian pedagogue, sir', and he would stride off, slamming the door, and loving it. He understood exactly how to run an Eton House.

The extension of Keate's Lane to the southwest towards South Meadow represents a Victorian and twentieth-century suburb of Eton, in which one can read the shifting of the school to meet modern subjects and the modern world.

First on the left is the **Natural History Museum** with bronze peacocks as the finials on its turrets, part of the **The Queen's Schools** opened by Queen Victoria in 1891, housing schoolrooms, laboratories, a large lecture hall and this museum. Reflecting the importance of science in a school which once despised it, the Science Schools were extended in 1903, again in the 1960s and again in the 1980s. In the 1860s, the great William Johnson,

author of the 'Eton Boating Song', had told a Royal
Commission investigating the state of the public schools
that geology could not be taught to boys without 'violent
disturbance' to their religious belief, and an attitude to
science probably typical of most Etonians was expressed
by the young Harold Macmillan to his mother on 6 June
1916:

> I am rather annoyed at the nonsense people are
> writing and talking about 'Education'....We are all
> to learn, it seems, about stocks and shares. Instead of
> humanities we are to dissect frogs and make horrible
> smells in expensive laboratories....I do not see that
> an ignorance of chemistry is any better than an
> ignorance of Classics.

Even in the 1930s, David Fraser's memory of his housemaster was that

> If one took an adverse report ...from a science
> master to Upcott he simply observed 'Oh, science!'
> and signed it with a yawn and without a second
> glance.

But there are also better traditions here, many of them
reflected in displays in the Natural History Museum,
built in memory of a boy who died in the Baldwin's

Shore fire. Alongside such curiosities as the giant flightless stuffed parrot from New Zealand, the two-faced cat and the four-footed duck, two biologists are commemorated.

The naval officer, Constantine Phipps, Nelson's early commander, was the first European to describe a polar bear (in 1774). His friend, the great Joseph Banks, for forty-one years president of the Royal Society, the botanist who accompanied Captain Cook on his first voyage to the South Seas, discovered hundreds of species unknown to the Europeans: *Eucalyptus*, bottlebrush, *Mimosa*, dazzling examples of the genus that came to be known as *Banksia* and the lemon yellow *Hibiscus tiliaceus*. In the museum there is a mock-up of his cabin on the *Endeavour*, and the flower-bed in the otherwise unattractive science quadrangle is planted entirely with *Banksiae*.

Banks had been a rather naughty boy at Eton. His tutor Edward Young had written to his father in February 1757:

> You can't but be sensible that there is a great Inattention in him, and an immoderate Love of Play. (I hope you will excuse my giving you my Opinion of Him so freely, as I cannot think it right to deceive you in a Point of so much Consequence to his Welfare.) This sometimes occasions Quarrels

between us; tho' in other respects we agree extremely well together, as I really think him a very good-tempered and well disposed Boy.

Banks was lax in attending to his Latin and Greek but spent his spare time botanising in this very lane where it stretches out towards the river. He paid the apothecaries' gatherers working here to tell him the names and purposes of the hedgerow plants they were picking. You can imagine the hilarity with which they took his money but this curious instinct was the foundation of the science of ethno-botany.

Three twentieth-century biologists who learned their science at Eton proved almost equally influential. Both Julian Huxley, an evolutionary biologist and later the first Director of UNESCO, and J.B.S. Haldane, a Marxist as well as one of the original proponents of the neo-Darwinian theory, were awarded the Darwin Medal, and John Gurdon, the first person to clone a frog, had the Wellcome Institute for Cell Biology and Cancer renamed the Gurdon Institute in his honour. After a visit to speak to the Scientific Society, James Watson of double-helix fame, for several years took on each year a young Etonian between school and university to work in a research team at his Cold Spring Harbor laboratories. So the life sciences tradition continues.

The most famous of Eton scientists was Robert Boyle,

author of *The Sceptical Chymist* and founder of modern chemistry. His father was a friend of Wotton's and Robert was sent to Eton in the 1630s when he was eight years old. He was a schoolboy workaholic, what would now be called a nerd, and his tutor Mr Harrison who 'instructed him privately and familiarly in his chamber' had to force him to go out and play, bestowing on him

> such balls and tops, and other implements of idleness, as he had taken away from others, that had unduly used them.

He left Eton after three years and went abroad with his tutor.

Other Eton scientists were Sir John Herschel the mathematician, Charles Rolls (whose collaborator was Royce), Robert Rayleigh who worked on radioactivity and Stephen Wolfram, creator of Mathematica, a revolutionary form of computer software, and advocate for *A New Kind of Science*, as he called his book, based on investigating how complexity in the universe emerges from simple logical systems. Twenty-four current Fellows of the Royal Society and the British Academy began their education at Eton.

The **Lower Chapel,** consecrated in 1891, is an unloved Victorian tribute to the perpendicular of College Chapel. As *The Times* put it in 1925, 'the interior of the chapel has not the beauty of the main Eton Chapel' but there are two good jokes on the memorials inside. On the north wall of the sanctuary there is a tablet which begins with a Greek text meaning 'He giveth grace to the humble', and continues in Latin as follows:

> Tom Cottingham Edwards-Moss was twice Captain of the Boats. His father and brother each in his year, also achieved this highest of Eton distinctions. After six very well behaved and irreproachable years at Eton he entered Brasenose, Oxford, where by his charm of manner he won the affection of his contemporaries. After leaving university he was chosen Member of Parliament for Widnes in Lancashire. There his loyalty, his earnestness, and his wisdom won the good will of all. Then after a sudden illness he fell asleep in Christ 16th December, 1893, in the 31st year of his age, thus disappointing the hopes of his friends.

Low on the south wall of the sanctuary, there is another inscription which (in Latin) seems to begin, 'You who in this chapel worship God, an Etonian like yourselves...' It takes a good Latinist reading as far as the fifth line to discover that it is not God but Major W.J. Myers who was the Etonian.

Beyond Lower Chapel is a vast barn of a boys' house

called **South Lawn** and beyond that the beautiful summer grass of South Meadow. Through it a foot-worn path leads down to the river which Joseph Banks and Shelley both liked to follow. Until the end of the nineteenth century, one could still see here 'at the northernmost point of South Meadow' the stump of a willow which Shelley had destroyed with fire in one of his magnifying-glass, pyromaniac wanderings.

The **Birley Schools** is the headquarters for language teaching, historically a low priority at Eton. In the mid-nineteenth century, there was one French master and an assistant for the school and it was generally thought that German and Italian could be effectually taught in school, but not French. As the assistant master Edward Coleridge said to his headmaster Dr Hawtrey

> Is there not something in the disposition of English boys so utterly repugnant to Frenchmen that it would be impossible to teach the French language in class?

A slightly strange remark: did it mean Etonians were repugnant to Frenchmen or vice versa? When French was introduced as a serious subject in 1864 the *Eton Chronicle*, edited by boys, leaves little doubt that it was the latter:

It is not, we understand, the present intention of those in authority to insist on the *speaking* of the language...

As for literature the productions of French authors are very generally a reflexion of the national character – artificial and shallow. At any rate it would be Quixotic to aim at acquiring a correct French accent except by actual intercourse with natives. It is for these reasons we hope that French will not fill too large a place in the education of the School.

There has been a complete reversal in recent years. More boys from Eton take modern languages at A-level than in any other school. German, Spanish, Russian, Italian, Arabic, Japanese, Mandarin, and sometimes Portuguese are on offer as well as French.

Next door are the **Music Schools,** opened in 1886 and doubled in size in the late 1990s. The Greek inscription over the doorway means 'God gave divine song'. Ralph Allwood, for twenty-five years the Precentor and Director of Music, has inspired divine song far beyond Eton by bringing the best young singers from all over the country to his Eton Summer Schools. If Eton boys want to learn an unconventional instrument like the ukelele, the steel drums or the didgeridoo, he will find them a teacher. More than half the boys in the school now learn one or more instruments, and there is a recording studio and control room, as well as computer technology rooms and a room, as the official *Eton Guide* puts it with its handkerchief to its nose, 'where boys, for a subscription, can play all kinds of loud and up-to-the-minute music without disturbing others.'

There is a long musical tradition. The composers Thomas Arne, Hubert Parry, George Butterworth, Roger Quilter and Peter Warlock were all boys at Eton. So was John Christie, the founder of Glyndebourne, and two early Artistic Directors of the Edinburgh Festival, Robert Ponsonby and Lord Harewood. Humphrey Lyttelton, Frances Grier, Jeremy Menuhin and Michael Chance were boys here, as well as a dozen former King's College Cambridge organists and a growing number of professional musicians. Of the dozen or so living composers who were at school at Eton some are writing 'up-to-the-minute' music for dance, television and films and one is a successful DJ.

At the corner, where the road swings up towards Eton Wick are the plain 1938 **Montague James Schools**, which are now the Classics department. At the suggestion of Stephen Spurr, the head of department and later Head Master of Westminster, the little formal garden behind is planted entirely with shrubs familiar to the Romans. The **Eton Wick Road,** is lined with Boys' Houses in a sort of orangey brick with vaguely Queen Anne revival elements plastered on.

First, though, on the left is **Bekynton,** the purpose-built dining room now used by half the Houses, designed by Powell and Moya, opened in 1972 and extended in 1980. The building is named after Bishop Bekynton, Secretary to Henry VI and an early patron of the College. It is thought to be efficient but looks flimsy.

Next to it is **Walpole House,** in so-called Queen Anne style, built in 1906-7. In the 1920s, this was A.M Goodhart's, 'not merely a "bad" house,' according to Anthony Powell who was a boy here, 'but universally agreed to be far the "worst" house in the school'.

We don't know which House Bertie Wooster or James Bond might have been in, but Walpole is the House in which you have to imagine Widmerpool, Powell's great creation, who surfaces in *A Question of Upbringing*, the first in the *Dance to the Music of Time* sequence, published in 1951.

On the other side of the road are two boarding-houses, **Waynflete and Westbury,** named for early Provosts who saved the College from Edward IV. They are said to be in 'a free domestic Tudor style,' both built in 1899-1900. In modern times Waynflete was the house of Paul Watkins the novelist. Watkins, who has won the Forward Prize and twice reached the Booker shortlist, describes his time at Eton in *Stand Before Your God*. He won the Headmaster's Short Story Prize (adjudicated that year by Susan Hill).

Mustians, on the left, completed in 1937 and **Cotton Hall House**, on the right, complete this unlovely quintet of solid, decent twentieth-century houses. Nowhere more than on the Eton Wick road does Eton look quite so much like a gathering of lumpen barracks. But the recipe of one boy per room is certainly a source of adolescent delight. 'Never will the new boy feel so grand again,' Bernard Fergusson wrote in the 1930s,

as when he looks on his Eton room for the first time. Here he will eat, sleep, work, rag, read, sing, and play the fool with his friends for many months to come.

First there is the bed, invisible by day, and occupying most of the room by night. By day it folds up against the wall, with curtains in front of it. Next we have the burry. The names of former owners are tastefully engraved in burnt pokerwork, and its drawers may yield mementoes of the past proprietor. A table, a wash-stand and a Windsor chair are the only other pieces provided. [Pre-modern Eton disliked armchairs and they were banned from boys' rooms.] An ottoman – a low square box with a padded top to sit on. In it will live a mixed collection of football boots, fives gloves, fives balls, footballs, football clothes, fives clothes, cricket clothes, rowing clothes, bathing drawers, corps clothes, cricket balls, batting gloves and sock.

No matter how small your room is, your friends will come crowding in, to pass the time of day, to prepare a construe [a set translation from Latin to English], or for tea.

It comes as some surprise to learn that Alec Douglas-Home, Captain of the Eleven in 1922, and Prime Minister, boarded in **Cotton Hall**. You would somehow expect to associate him with a Palladian villa or a country-house with wellington-boots inside the front door, but when he arrived here in 1917, he found a house overlooking a graveyard, running with rats and where he was fed something called 'Miss Martin's pudding which consisted of cold suet and bacon fat.' It wouldn't be allowed nowadays.

At the end of the narrow paved pathway alongside Cotton Hall **Farrer Ho**use (1959) and beyond it down a side passage, **Villiers House** (1962), both designed by Lord Holford, continue the modern Eton tradition of effortlessly inadequate architecture: lots of little effects with brick and slate, no overall presence, buildings which seem to have been left over from the Festival of Britain. The wings of Farrer House are curved so that the corridors inside don't feel like a prison. It has a nuclear bunker underneath, but who was meant to go in it when the missiles came in? When the boys came first to live in the House, they hated it. Nicholas Monson, who was here in 60s, called it 'an animated filing cabinet':

> Ghastly hideous place, it was a nightmare. Talk about the traditions of Eton. I mean I could have been anywhere. I could have been in Nevada.

Boys like it now.

A hundred yards past Farrer House, on the corner of Common Lane, is the big grey-brick block of **Warre House**, built in the 1840s by John Hawtrey. He housed all the smallest boys here in what was in effect a prep school for Eton. The Lower Boys all ate here together and had their own playing field next door. It was a private business and the school did not acquire the house or its site until 1906. This is the house where Humphrey Lyttelton, whose father was Housemaster here, practised the trumpet in the basement, and in which David Cameron boarded between 1979 and 1984. Across Common Lane, once known also as Cow Lane (it is the route out to the grazing on the common) or Gasworks Lane, from the gasworks which once stood on the site of the **Parade Ground,** are the severe Edwardian red-brick walls of the Alington and Caxton Schools and the ridged concrete façade of the **Farrer Theatre.**

This is not a pretty place. If you compare it with School Yard, created in the fifteenth and sixteenth centuries, it is a disgrace: utilitarian, charmless, horrible materials, looking like the back-end of the gasworks it once was. You could make a film about Austerity Britain here. Why are we so bad at this? Enormous improvements are made to the interiors of buildings – their comfort, technology, warmth – but the public spaces are left as orphans and widows. The Farrer Theatre, the only concrete building in a square of brick, was built between 1966 and 1968. The hideous concrete ripple cladding was designed to exclude the noise of aeroplanes, which it does. The interior is however functional and efficient.

Etonians seem to enjoy the sound of their own voices. Plays were performed in Long Chamber in College very early; the Tudor headmaster Nicholas Udall wrote the earliest surviving comedy in English (*Ralph Roister Doister* – of which the unique copy is in College Library) and nowadays boys perform two dozen plays a year, here or in the Caccia Studio or the Other Space in the next–door building. Some go on to make a career of it: Charles Kean may have been the lone Etonian actor of note in the nineteenth century, but more than a dozen have followed in his footsteps in recent years. Eddie Redmayne and Tom Hiddleston have won Olivier awards and Redmayne a Tony Award as well. Three other have been the stars of American television blockbusters: Hugh Lawrie in *House*,

Damian Lewis in *Band of Brothers* and Dominic West in *The Wire*. Unfortunately John Gielgud did not come to Eton. He disqualified himself – he self-deprecatingly admitted – by scoring 0% in maths in the entry exam.

At the end of the Parade Ground are the **Drawing Schools** (1921, extended in 1977-9, 1986, 1997 and 2002), an enormous building which replaces the Evanses' little studio in Keate's Lane. Inside are areas for painting, screen-printing, sculpture and ceramics (this last under the direction for many years of Gordon Baldwin, the internationally-known potter). When John Booth was Drawing Master in the eighties and nineties the Drawing Schools attracted unprecedented numbers of boys in their spare time, a mixture of serious artists, boys who just found painting fun and others who came mainly for the good talk and the putting of the world to rights. It was a little centre of civilization. Many people now running galleries or working in the auction houses had part of their education here and at least a dozen of their contemporaries have become successful professional artists.

At one time this was the stamping-ground and kingdom of Wilfrid Blunt, art master from 1938 until 1959, the brother of Anthony Blunt, the connoisseur and spy (who was not at Eton). In his spectacularly indiscreet and witty memoir *Slow on the Feather*, Wilfrid blows the gaff on his particular, rather queeny corner of Eton life, discussing both his own infatuations with boys and the sad and sometimes obsessive behaviour of other boy-loving masters. It can't always have been easy. The siting of the Drawing Schools next to the Parade Ground, on which the Officer Training Corps drilled, 'often led to open warfare' and the relationship wasn't helped during the real war by Blunt's own performance as a member of what he liked to call the Strike Force of Eton's Home Guard. Blunt saw little action apart from having once 'shot a cow which had not responded to my challenge.'

For all his self-deprecation, Blunt was an inspirational teacher to generations of boys. He reckoned he had nurtured something over ten thousand, none of whom he could ever remember even when they remembered him:

> When I am accosted in Piccadilly by some ancient white-bearded bishop who addresses me as 'sir', I am not always able to recognise what remains of some cherub of the Twenties. Occasionally, however, when the name of one of them catches the headlines, I recall an infant. There was a bright little new boy at Eton in the Fifties named Sir Ranulph Twistelton-Wykeham-Fiennes. 'I can't call you all that,' I said. 'Will "Fiennes" do?' 'Just call me Twinkletoes,' he said.

Fiennes says this is 'sheer invention'. He says his nickname was 'Sir Griswold' and Blunt must have misheard it.

Among all the explorers, diplomats, generals and bankers who passed through his hands, there was, in Howard Hodgkin, one artist of world standing. Hodgkin was at Eton for only eighteen months in 1945-6 and hated it, as he hated all schools, but Blunt was an oasis of difference. 'He could have taught a programme of concentrated wickedness,' Hodgkin has said, 'and we would have gone along with it.' Blunt introduced Hodgkin to Mughal and Rajput miniatures, which he has collected ever since, and whose intensity of colour-effects and non-western perspectives lie behind much of his life's work. He came back to open the newest extension to the building, because of his memories of Wilfrid Blunt.

As Common Lane curves back towards the centre of the school, Eton's twentieth-century suburbia gives way to the look and feel of a small English town. On the right are two boys' houses, the first **Penn House** (1860), the second **Common Lane House**, hugely extended in 1870. Between the two on the same side is **2 Common Lane**, a 'colony' for bachelor masters. At the end of World War I, the enormously rich but wounded John Christie was a physics master at his old school. As his private staff he had a groom, a chauffeur and a butler, the last of whom he occasionally sent to meet the boys at 7.30 for early school: 'Captain Christie will be along presently, gentlemen,' the poor man was told to announce to them. Under Christie's leadership, 2 Common Lane became known as 'Liqueur Cottage' because of the variety of bottles on display.

When passing Common Lane House, it is easy to miss the sculpture by Antony Gormley of a man, anchored by his feet and looking down on you from the horizontal, twenty-five feet above. This cast of Gormley's body, called Edge II, was put up in 2002. For a school keenly interested in rank, relative position and the long strive upwards, his presence above the street is a reminder of another way of looking at the world.

On the other side of the road, are the **Warre Schools** (1904) on the site of the Angelos' Fencing and Dancing School. Behind them stands the Boys' House called Angelo's after Domenick Angelo's daughter Sophia who became a Dame while still under twenty. She used to wear an ermine tippet, drove out in a pony and chaise, was styled the Duchess of Eton and 'to the end of her days used patch and powder and wore ringlets.'

Rory Stewart was a boy in this House from 1986-91. He is the latest in Eton's line of adventurers which includes Aubrey Herbert ('the man who was Greenmantle'), Denys Finch-Hatton of *Out of Africa*, Wilfred Thesiger and Ranulph Fiennes. He has walked across Asia, been deputy-governor of a province in Iraq and won the Hawthornden Prize.

The last House on the left is the **Hopgarden,** a boarding-house built by the Rev. T. Carter about 1823, looking rather like a vicarage, incorporating an earlier cottage and like every other Eton House repeatedly added to. Anthony Eden, later Prime Minister, boarded here in an almost totally undistinguished Eton career. As his biographer puts it, 'he was never one of its golden boys'.

Perhaps most Etonians only become Etonian after they have left.

Two holders of the VC and three of the MC were in this house in the twenties. It was believed that all five had by chance lived in the same room, but when they came back to visit they were divided about which room it was – not surprising perhaps if you consider that boys change room every year and that the house was substantially remodelled in the eighties. It was the Housemaster here, with whom he had climbed while a boy at school, that Bear Grylls, at that time the youngest man to climb Everest, telephoned from the summit. Mike Town reminded him that more people die on the way down than on the way up. Grylls descended safely.

In the old core of the village of Eton and on the corner of Common Lane is **Manor House**, on the site of a long-disappeared medieval manor house but most famous recently as the House in which Princes William and Harry boarded between 1995 and 2004. Both, on the whole, had the most typical of times there, doing adequately at work, enjoying games (William swimming, Harry the Wall Game) and not surprisingly doing well socially (William in Pop, Harry not). When Harry was eighteen a photograph of his room in Manor House was published and extensively analysed in *The Guardian*:

> Harry's photographs show the 6ft 2in prince surrounded by a few of his favourite things, which include pin-ups of two admired women. Wonderbra model Caprice was said by her agent yesterday to be 'chuffed to bits' to be one of them, while the opinion of the actor Halle Berry was not known. Also on Harry's desk is a bottle of his father's Duchy Originals mineral water, and a favourite portrait of his mother, Princess Diana, by Mario Testino.

But all was not entirely plain sailing. One summer evening, the fast bowler of the Eleven was playing corridor cricket with a junior boy on the top floor of Manor House. He bowled him a bouncer which went over the boy's head and straight through the window behind him. By chance, at exactly that moment, some other boys in the neighbouring Godolphin House, also playing on a summer's evening, threw a fire-cracker out of the window. It landed, again by chance, next to one of the Manor House dailies who had just parked her car below them.

It went off, she screamed and the combined impression of the fire-cracker, the smashed window and the scream convinced the royal security officers that Manor House was under attack. The Housemaster, Andrew Gailey, and his wife, Shauna, were having a dinner-party on the ground floor:

> The first we knew that something was up was the sight of balaclavaed men with machine-guns racing through the hall on to the boys' side. I rather left them to it and the next we knew of it was the sight at my dining-room door of the poor boys coming to apologize surrounded by these armed police. Needless to say my guests were agog – I hoped at the seriousness with which Eton took matters of discipline.

In fact the boys were not punished because the House-master had a rule that boys were not to be had up for anything coming to light through the security arrangements necessary to guard the princes.

This was the House, run by a family called the Ragueneaus, in which the Duke of Wellington had boarded as the lonely, lazy and awkward Arthur Wesley in the 1780s. He returned as the victor of Waterloo in January 1818:

The Duke came to Mr Ragueneau's. He went all over the house and visited the room which he had occupied when at school. He looked into the garden, and asked what had become of the broad black ditch over which he used so often to leap. He said 'I really believe I owe my spirit of enterprise to the tricks I used to play in the garden.'

It is just possible that the apocryphal dictum about the battle of Waterloo being won on the playing-fields of Eton — never said by the Duke but a treasured nostrum of the Victorian ruling-class — had its origin in those words. The Duke had two sons at the school, Lord Douro and Lord Charles Wellesley (the spelling of the name had changed) and on this visit Dr Keate, then headmaster, 'saw him coming down the lane holding his two boys by the hand,' an unexpectedly touching sight. The Duke took a stroll through School Yard, a celebrity, and was cheered by the boys.

But the two boys, particularly the younger, did not impress their father. This terrifying letter arrived at Eton on October 23 1824 when Charles was 16:

> In respect of your idleness it is your own affair, and I shall observe but little upon it. I have done my duty by you. I have spared neither trouble nor expence to give you the best education that this

country could afford, in hopes that you might at least keep your place among your equals, if not some time or other be able to distinguish yourself. It is your own fault if you have not availed yourself of the opportunities which have been afforded to you for improvement. You are now of an age to be able to feel all the consequences of your idleness, and I therefore take the opportunity of warning you that you will live in times when your Ignorance will be a perpetual drawback upon you, and that no power on earth will be able to place you in any excepting the lowest situations unless you should be qualified to fill higher, by your diligence, your acquirements and your duties.

Believe me, ever most affly.

W

Can affection ever have been quite so cold? As it turned out, Charles became a Major-General, a long-standing Tory MP and a favourite member of Queen Victoria's household. His elder brother was a nonentity. On succeeding to his father's titles, he remarked sadly, 'Think what it will be when the Duke of Wellington is announced, and only I walk into the room...'

To the right of Manor House, and a little set back, is the redbrick **Godolphin House** with 1722, the date of its building, on a rainwater head. It is named after

Henry Godolphin, the Provost who gave School Yard its statue of the Founder. Godolphin is famous as the House in which A.C. Benson, one of Eton's most distinguished and subtle-minded of men, was Housemaster.

A slightly ridiculous blue plaque is fixed to the wall, saying that A.C.Benson, Housemaster from 1899-1903, was the author of 'Land of Hope and Glory', which indeed he was, at the request of Edward VI. He tossed off the lines for a Coronation Ode in 1902, to accompany Elgar's *Pomp and Circumstance March No. 1*. In doing so he became yet another Etonian to write the words or music of a popular national song, joining Thomas Arne who wrote 'Rule Britannia' and 'God Save the King', Parry who set 'Jerusalem' to music and Cecil Spring-Rice, the author of 'I vow to thee my Country'.

But Benson was more than the author of the anthem of the Conservative Party. He recorded in his diary the moment he arrived:

> One of the most *amenable* houses in Eton. The garden, with the huge old Spanish chestnut is very pleasant to look out on – the birds piped loud there the first morning I went and stood out on the balcony, and the screen of lilacs is so contrived it hides all walls and buildings…I seem to look right away over country, seeing the forms of tall trees

further and further down to the horizon – and to be joined to the garden of Eden.

It was not all paradise:

> We are here (1) a maitre d'hôtel (2) a clergyman (3) a lecturer (4) a coach (5) a policeman – most of us are athletes too – and [the Head Master] has made many reforms and *all* have added to the masters' work and responsibilities.

Modern Housemasters have been known to say much the same.

Another writer was associated with the House, as a boy not a beak. William Fiennes won the Hawthornden Prize with his first book, *The Snow Geese*.

To the right of Godolphin House is **Holland House**, one of the most delightful of Eton Houses, with a huge garden, where John Keate lived before becoming Head Master. In modern times a young old boy of the House called Marcus Armytage, given a late ride because a jockey was unavailable, became the last amateur to win the Grand National.

Across the road **New Schools** (they were new in 1861) were built on the site of a wild and chaotic Pig Fair held every Ash Wednesday. The yard in front of New Schools is called Cannon Yard after a gun captured at Sebastopol during the Crimean War and given by General Peel, the War Secretary, in 1867. It was in these schools in March 1891 that Gladstone made his great speech on Homer.

Here too, rather less successfully, Aldous Huxley taught at the end of World War I. He had briefly been in College in 1908-11 and returned as a master in the war-diminished circumstances of 1917-19. His brilliance was unquestioned. Asked as a boy to write down everything he knew about the conquistadors, he produced:

> It's my settled belief that Pissarro
> Must have been educated at Harro
> This alone would suffice
> To account for his vice
> And his morals so scroobious and narro

But inflammation of the cornea in 1911, *keratitis punctata,* left him nearly blind and the boys of 1917 were merciless. One of them was the poet Eddy Sackville-West:

> Poor Aldous! He must have been one of the most incompetent schoolmasters who ever faced a class.....his solution was to read aloud, with occasional comments the poems of Verlaine. This he did in his scholarly, highly modulated voice... [It was] impossible to hear more than an occasional

word of what he read or said for the general tumult was indescribable. Those in the back row but one turned their backs on the rest of the form and made up a bridge four with boys in the back row. The middle rows played noughts-and-crosses with white chalk on the shoulders of the boys in front of them.....From time to time, Aldous would pause, look up, and say, in an imploring tone, 'Oh! Do be quiet!' No one took the slightest notice.

For all that, as Sackville-West acknowledged, Huxley managed to introduce him to Laforgue and Mallarmé, which remained formative influences for the rest of his life. Another boy, the future historian of the Crusades, Sir Steven Runciman, remembered with affection

that elongated, stooping myopic figure, with a face that was far younger than most of our masters [Huxley was 23] and yet seemed somehow ageless, and usually hidden by an infinite variety of spectacles, eyes that were almost sightless and yet almost uncomfortably observant. He stood there looking something of a martyr but at the same time extraordinarily distinguished.

And Eric Blair, amid the din, kept his pencil poised to note down the fine phrase or two that Huxley would inevitably utter, the future author of *1984* taught by the future author of *Brave New World*. Eton figures briefly in *Brave New World,* with a ferro-concrete sky-scraper where Lupton's Tower once stood, a Community Singery on the site of the Chapel and a headmistress called Miss Keate.

The block running out behind, at right angles to the original New Schools, was built in 1876 and called the 'New-new Schools'. It is properly known as the New Mathematical Schools, and was enlarged with an unob-trusive extra storey in 2001. The Computer department was housed at the same time in a squat modern addition, popularly known as the Bunker and universally loathed. It is almost exactly on the site of 'a hot roll and sock shop, kept by three sisters' called Spiers. Shelley told his friend Rees Howell Gronow that Martha Spiers 'was the loveli-est girl I ever saw, and I loved her to distraction.'

There are four Boys' Houses you tend to miss on a walk through Eton. Looking on to the Field are **Wotton House** and the **Timbralls**, whose site was the timber-yard for much early construction at Eton. Tucked behind the churchyard is **Baldwin's Bec**, which was rebuilt after the war and is next to Baldwin's Shore, the Boys' House gutted by fire in 1902. Two boys were burnt to death. If there had been no bars across their windows, they might have climbed down the vast wisteria to safety and since then there have been no bars across boys' windows anywhere in Eton. On the other side of the High Street is the oldest of the Houses, **Jourdelays**, purchased in 1441 for the fledgling college. It was George III's favourite Eton house and he always recommended it to prospective parents. But all that has gone. It was altered in 1864-6, again in 1974 and again in 2005. Beau Brummell boarded here, "a very *clever* and a very *idle* boy" whom "Nature seemed to have supplied... with a quadruple portion of amusing repartee."

Finally, at the very centre of Eton, across the road from the entrance to School Yard and the College stand two big memorial buildings, **School Library** and **School Hall**, both built from 1902 – 1908 by subscription among Old Etonians as a memorial to the one hundred and twenty-nine Etonians killed in the Boer War. Nothing of the kind would have been possible after World War I. On the day of the Armistice in November 1918, a large group of Etonians marched to the room of the Commander of the Officer Training Corps and demanded his resignation now that peace had come. Too many had died. The old men were too stupid. College became 'Bolshie'. Fifteen out of sixteen boys in the Headmaster's Division in 1920 included Lenin among a list of the ten greatest men alive. One of them was the Colleger later known as George Orwell.

Against all this, the pompous Edwardian baroque pieties of School Library and School Hall, designed and conceived by a 'Committee of Taste' that was widely ridiculed even at the time, looked ironic and misplaced to that later generation.

The new buildings replaced a jumble of sock shops including Mother Hatton's popina, a joiner's, a grocer's, and some Boys' Houses, in one of which Shelley charged the door handle to his room with electricity, giving the master who came to ask about the noise of the machine an unpleasant shock.

Passing School Hall in mid-morning you are likely to find the steps and pavement thronged with boys waiting to waylay a beak with whom they have business. Inside the masters assemble for twenty minutes to hear the notices given out by the Head Master and any of their number with information that needs to be broadcast to all. This must be the only school where the masters' morning break is devoted to a masters' meeting rather than a cup of coffee, but in a large dispersed school there is huge convenience for beaks in knowing that the person they need to see will be in School Hall for those twenty minutes and, for boys, in having the chance of catching the beak they need to see as he goes in or out of 'Chambers'. (It is called that because in earlier centuries the small teaching staff met in the Head Master's chamber, the room where the wall-painting of the schoolroom in the sixteenth-century was discovered.)

Otherwise School Hall is used for assemblies, concerts and examinations. Matthew Pinsent spoke there four years after sitting in the audience himself as a boy. He passed round his Olympic gold medal, saying 'Just hand it back when it reaches the end of the last row.' One morning assembly was enlivened by another young Old Etonian speaker who, to catch his audience's attention, brought a four-foot python on to the stage. It slipped away and at the end could not be found. Within ten minutes a tabloid had asked the Head Master to confirm that there was a man-eating snake loose at Eton. The situation was saved, and the disaster the tabloid hoped for averted, by the master-in-charge of the assembly, Barnaby Lenon, who found the reptile under a seat cushion, popped it in a bag and left it in the front hall of the Lower Master's house. He later became Head Master of Harrow.

Outside, stands the decorative wrought-iron lamp-post known as the **Burning Bush**. It was originally designed to stand in New Schools Yard, but the Russian cannon displaced it, and it was placed instead in the middle of the Slough Road. When an island was made to allow boys to cross in safety, the Burning Bush was moved to its present site west of the road. It is the meeting-place for boys, outside speakers or other visitors arriving in Eton.

Here, at the end of the summer term in the early 19th century, you would have seen the Regency swells leaving for the holidays. Today if you take a taxi from Slough Station and ask for Eton, the taxi-driver invariably replies, 'Burning Bush?'

CHAPTER FOUR

WESTON'S YARD AND
THE FIELDS

THE NAME OF ETON, its etymology long forgotten, means 'the river farm', the *Ea-tun*. Now the Thames is tamed and controlled but in the early years of Saxon England, the centre of Eton, where the Chapel stands across from the Manor House, was on a little island surrounded by the netted, braided, marshy streams of the river. It runs today under Windsor bridge between its chartered banks and then past Fellows' Eyot on its way to the Home Park, Datchet, Staines and London.

To reach the river it is easiest to go through the little Victorian Gothic arch into **Weston's Yard**, on the other side of the main road from School Hall. Like a lesser School Yard, this space is framed by different eras. Backing on to the Slough road is **Savile House**, originally 17th-century but smashed by a bomb in the war and rebuilt afterwards. Facing it are the 1840s **New Buildings**, part of the great mid-Victorian humanisation of Collegers' lives, and to the right is the fifteenth-century range, exactly four hundred years earlier, of the original, brutal accommodation for scholars, with the **Long Chamber** on the first floor, Lower School and the Master-in-College's study below. It is a hybrid place, partly of the College, partly of the school clustering beyond it. This is the route out to the playing fields and during term time in the afternoon there is a stream of boys flowing to or from the pitches.

It wasn't always so *soigné*. Every summer until 1747, on the election of the new scholars, an extraordinarily primitive ram-hunt was conducted by the boys, beginning here. At least from the 1680s, every summer, the College butcher had to provide a ram and the boys were charged 9d on their bill for membership of the 'Bat & Ram Club.' In August 1730, the Duke of Cumberland, a nine-year-old younger son of George II and sixteen years later the vastly fat destroyer of the Jacobites, came over from Windsor to take part:

> The Captain of the School presented him with a ram-club, with which H.R.H. struck the first stroke. H.R.H. was in at the death of the ram, and his club was bloodyed according to custom.

It was on one of these occasions that an active ram crossed the Thames and ran through the market-place at Windsor with the young hunters in full cry after it. Such severe

'A way of life rather than a job.' A House Master with his wife, the Dame and his boys.

First morning at Eton: few things seem more complicated than learning to tie the tie.

Eton independence. Your own room decorated according to your own taste.

'An awful lot of work to do:' beaks stay in their own schoolrooms and boys move round.

The dining-room in a modern House (top) and College Hall with collegers' gowns hung against the panelling. Mutton, bread and beer were the staple diet until Victorian times.

A boy 'in the Bill', summoned to account for himself in the austere surroundings of the Head Master's schoolroom.

'Working under the shadow of the great men that have gone before.' End of term exams or 'Trials' in Upper School.

'Chambers', the daily masters' meeting, on this occasion held in Upper School.

A beak waylaid outside Chambers.

Part-jolly, part-anxious boating weather on the Fourth of June.

'God gave divine song.' The Precentor and some of the Chapel choir.

'A slow, violent scramble in the mud': the St Andrew's Day Wall Game between Collegers in purple and white and Oppidans in purple and orange.

Back from the playing fields.

exercise in summer was deemed dangerous to the health of the boys, so thenceforth the unfortunate rams were hamstrung, and, after the regular speech, deliberately beaten to death in Weston's Yard. The custom became so utterly barbarous after this alteration, that it was finally abolished in 1747; but as late as 1760 a ram was served up in pasties at the high table in hall, at the great dinner on Election Monday.

Savile House, elegant behind its garden walls, was built between 1603 and 1606, part of it a house in which the Provost Henry Savile and several later Head Masters lived. Other parts of Savile House were rented by chaplains, clerks and the grander Oppidans. In the middle of the eighteenth century the Duke of Marlborough rented one of the houses for his sons and their tutor to live in, (the Marquess of Hertford rented one across the Slough road) and in the nineteenth century, the beautiful Arthur Hallam boarded here, in the house of the Head Master Edward Hawtrey. Every other morning – at least when their friendship was going well, which it sometimes didn't – Gladstone had breakfast with Hallam here; otherwise Hallam had breakfast with Gladstone in his rooms in Corner House beyond the Chapel.

In 1885 the building narrowly escaped demolition and was only saved by a coalition of William Morris-inspired masters, but in 1940 a German bomb exploded on impact in the centre of the range. Fred How, a master here at the time, describes what happened:

> Henry Ley, the Precentor, then occupied the whole length of Savile House; the dining-room was in the middle with the kitchen at one end of it and a small sitting-room at the other. The parlour-maid had just come through to the sitting-room to tell the Leys that dinner was ready; she then returned to the kitchen. Mrs Ley got up to go into the dining-room but Henry detained her for a moment to show her a joke in *Punch* which he was reading. It was during this moment that the bomb demolished the empty dining-room.

There were no casualties but the house was gutted by fire. After the war it was rebuilt to look, as far as possible, the same on the outside, but internally was divided into three smaller houses now lived in by masters.

Very different are the buildings on the far side of the yard. Immediately opposite is the hard, purple-red brick and black diapering of **New Buildings**, built in 1844-6 as an addition to College to provide better accommodation (but still no baths) for the miserable scholars who until then had been housed only in the medieval conditions of **Long Chamber**. So horrible were those conditions that before the improvements College was only half full. Partly this was because of the squalor to which no parents would happily expose their child and partly because the conditions were so bad that scholars had the added expense of a Dame's House out in the town where they could eat properly and have some privacy and comfort. The point of New Buildings, allied to a new and competitive entrance exam, was to make College attractive again to the cleverest boys in the country. It was Hodgson, on becoming Provost in 1840, who said, 'Please God, I will do something for those poor boys.'

The life of a Colleger in the one hundred and seventy-two feet of Long Chamber had been horrible, 'a rough barrack,' as one old Colleger remembered it in the 1840s. Boys were locked in Long Chamber from 6.30 pm at night till the next morning with practically no supervision. Another boy remembered it 'with the horror of pandemonium.' A scholar giving evidence to the Royal Commission investigating Eton in 1861 told it that the elder boys 'in punishing them did not use sticks, but usually boxed boys' ears or hit them with their fists.' The filth was so bad that visitors could rarely be shown the room. Each boy had a thin flock mattress; three blankets, thin also; sheets, bolster, no pillow; and a woollen horse-rug woven in long worsted strings for a counterpane.

Food was both bad and scarce, the source of old boys' bravado stories:

> A sow, very near her accouchement, had been observed by the boys feeding in Weston's Yard, close to the dormitory, when a most mischievous thought occurred, that she might be made useful to some of the community. The thought was no sooner devised than means as speedily used to put it in execution. One boy was directed to keep the animal feeding in a particular corner until dark. The scheme succeeded admirably; by throwing one of their cloth gowns over the old lady's snout, to obscure her vision, as well as to confine her squeaking trumpet from giving too much tongue, immediately, by the exertions of four stout boys, and no easy matter either, she was landed on the top of a tower, attached to Long Chamber: here she was regularly fed until some little piggy-wiggies came to light; which, as soon as they were considered to be of sufficient age, dangled before the fire in Chamber, and afforded the captors delicious suppers. As soon as the young fry had all paid the forfeit of their lives, for venturing to make their appearance within the precincts of the tower, the mamma was sent about her business, to seek old quarters, minus offspring.

Believe it if you will. Tennyson, whose brother was in College, put the story into verse.

When not too hungry, the scholars distracted themselves with plays, whose stage scenery and costumes were elaborate (one boy 'rode up and down Long Chamber on a donkey, which we had carried upstairs, in the full dress of the Life Guards') and other games. Rat-hunts gave some boys their happiest memories. The great eighteenth-century Greek scholar, Richard Porson, a poor boy from Norfolk, described how to catch a Long Chamber rat by stuffing a rolled-down sock into its empty hole, waiting for the rat to crawl in and then killing it by swinging the rat-stuffed sock against an iron bedstead. The dead rat would be skinned, and the skin pinned up as a trophy. The innards went under the floorboards. Sometimes beds were turned on end, with small boys inside; teams of boys tossed the smallest of their number in a blanket to see if he could touch the ceiling and attempts were made to throw cricket balls from one end of Long Chamber to the other, without touching ceiling, floor or walls.

It was the realm of small boy sadness and large boy tyranny. It is scarcely surprising that when George Canning, the future Prime Minister, was elected to College, Charles James Fox persuaded him to remain an Oppidan, a choice still occasionally made, one hopes for other reasons, by modern scholarship winners.

The addition of the New Buildings by Provost Hodgson allowed the number of boys in Chamber to be reduced to twenty-one in 1846, further reduced to fifteen in 1863. At the same time the room was divided into 'stalls' or cubicles.

In 1967, all that was tidied away and the interior of Long Chamber was rebuilt. The floor was raised four or five feet to put the windows at a usual height, central heating was provided, as well as basins in each room with hot and cold water. At last, every Colleger had his own room.

Not that College became integrated with the rest of the school. It remained a distinctly different place. The actor Patrick MacNee, an Oppidan in the thirties, remembers that 'freaks were scholars, basically, people who had too many brains, and were looked down on because they didn't pay.'

The contempt was not one-way. College has traditionally loathed, for example, the Corps. Quintin Hogg, later the Lord Chancellor Lord Hailsham, thought that the relationship between Collegers and Oppidans was 'a mutual dis-admiration.' They habitually looked down on each other and very occasionally fought (on the Long Walk.) But you only have to listen to Hogg's own estimation of himself to understand what it was the Oppidans had to put up with:

> I acquired, and have retained, an almost unlimited capacity to absorb information, great power of concentration, and meticulous habits of scholarship, marred only by the occasional carelessness caused by the speed at which I work. I was academically exceptionally gifted, and being intensely ambitious and competitive by nature, made full use of this gift. As I was rather cleverer than my contemporaries, I suppose I wasn't particularly popular.

Perhaps not. Unveiling his portrait at Eton as Lord Chancellor he poked fun at his juvenile self, maintaining that the great merit of College was that it knocked the bumptiousness out of you.

The High Court judge Michael Burton, a King's Scholar in the sixties, loved College because it was 'a university for teenagers', a tolerant place quite different from the Oppidan Houses where, as in the thirties, it was still necessary to be good at games and not to be thought a swot. College was the only musical House. There was no question of snobbery or bullying and not even any enforcement of lights-out.

Collegers often say in later life that they think of themselves as Collegers first and Etonians only second. The later years of the twentieth century, though, saw some rapprochement between Collegers and Oppidans.

Collegers behaved more like Oppidans, competing with them athletically as well as attempting to dominate them intellectually. Oppidans, many of them anyway, became more like Collegers. Of the eighty or so places won each year at Oxford and Cambridge, all on academic merit, nearly seventy go to Oppidans. With so many clever boys in the Oppidan houses Collegers no longer dominate the top divisions, in which Collegers and Oppidans now mix and mingle. The taunt that Collegers are paid for and Oppidans not is blurred too. There are more bursaries for Oppidans, and Collegers qualify automatically for only 10% of the fee, the rest, as for Oppidans, being made up if necessary by bursary money after a means test.

At the north-east end of Weston's Yard is the old beamy house called **Weston's**. House and yard are both named after Stephen Weston, an obscure master and Fellow who lived here in the early 1700s. The house was largely built in the seventeenth century, on the site of the almshouse prescribed by Henry VI as part of the Foundation, where 'thirteen poor weak men are always and for all future times to abide and remain.' They had been dispensed with as early as 1468, and from the seventeenth century onwards this was a Boys' House. It accommodated 'Turnip' Townshend, the Whig politician whose favourite conversational topic was 'that kind of rural improvement

which arises from turnips'; Dr Johnson's friend Topham
Beauclerk ('Sir, I would walk to the extent of the diameter
of the earth to save Beauclerk,' Dr Johnson said when he
heard he was dying); Horace Walpole; and Lord North,
the Prime Minister whose two distinctions were to have
lost the American colonies and to have been graced with
the finest leg in London. He was here with his brother
Brownlow, whom Lord North made a bishop at thirty.
'He is no doubt young', said Lord North, 'to be a bishop;
but when he is older he will not have his brother as Prime
Minister.'

Through the archway at the northern end of Weston's
Yard the road heads out to the playing fields. To the right,
where the Provost's stables used to be, is the **King of
Siam's Garden**, the present of an old boy of that name
to the school. To bored tourists Provost M.R. James
usually described a bronze figure of Perseus here, the
work of the Hungarian Lajos Strobl, as Henry VIII with
the head of Ann Boleyn. Next to it is a wall bearing the
inscription *Novi Fundatores* ('New Founders'). The names
engraved on it are those of Eton benefactors who have
made particularly generous contributions to the school
since 2005.

Where the road curves round to the left lie the original
playing fields of Eton referred to as the 'Playing mede'
as early as 1468. Horman's 1519 book of phrases to be

translated by Eton boys into Latin includes the sentence: 'We wyll pley with a ball full of wynde' and this first pitch is where they would have done so. It is called **College Field** and Collegers play on it today. Beyond it is the famous wall (built in 1717) against which, since at least the 1830s, the **Wall Game** has been played, largely by Collegers. It is a Michaelmas term game but all year long you can see the smear on the bricks where the muddy boys in the scrum or 'bully' have rubbed up against the wall.

'As a spectator sport,' the Californian writer and Old Colleger Pico Iyer thought, 'the Wall Game ranks somewhere between tortoise-racing and grass-growing.' It is played along a narrow strip (three hundred and fifty-five feet by fifteen) next to the wall. At the north end the goal is painted in white on a young tree, an end known as Bad Calx (meaning bad chalk); the goal at the other end, Good Calx, is the door into the garden of Weston's, which is easier to hit, hence Good. It is also nearer, in this wilfully eccentric game, the so-called halfway mark.

As Pico Iyer has described, 'it is usually a rather slow, violent scramble in the mud,'

> a many-legged frenzy that resembles the death throes of some monstrous crab. The players in the bully try to move toward the goal by clutching the

ball between their ankles and hopping through the mess of enemy forces, all the while keeping the ball in contact with the Wall. This is not much harder than balancing an egg on one's nose while crawling through the trenches of Verdun. Far behind the bully, the other two players on each team stand around idly, painting their fingernails. If the ball makes one of its biennial appearances outside the bully, the job of these 'behinds' is to lumber up to it and kick it toward the opponents' goal. This happens with the frequency of lunar eclipses. Scoring is therefore virtually impossible. But the beauty of the Wall Game is that it makes a mockery of the very notions of victory and defeat.

Pointless then? Not at all.

It is a heroic game. Hubert Parry gloried in it. Anthony Powell's housemaster, A.M. Goodhart, recommended to him 'an old tail coat' as the best outfit for the game. George Orwell distinguished himself with play described in the official Wall Game report as 'conspicuously bad.' Ian Fleming had his nose broken while playing it against Henry Douglas-Home, the Prime Minister's brother. Lord Hailsham, playing for College, was bitten on the leg during the annual St Andrews' Day match against the Oppidans by the 7th Duke of Montrose, a white supremacist and anti-Semite. He ended up as a minister in Ian Smith's Rhodesian government and came to think that the Beatles were agents of a communist plot to dominate the world.

Apparently the Wall Game can now be studied as part of the GCSE in Sports Studies. As a result two northern schools have challenged Eton to games. These were keenly contested and fortunately no accident occurred. The Risk Assessment Form filled in by the visitors for their local authorities was at first deemed inadequate as it failed to address the risk of a spectator falling off the top of the wall and injuring a player below.

Good Calx was also the 'milling ground' where, until the mid-nineteenth century and the surge in organised games, the boys settled their scores with bare-knuckled fist-fights. Late afternoon was the usual time, and it was said that the London coaches coming along the Slough road used to stop to let their passengers watch.

Here is an extract from *The London Chronicle* of December 7 1784:

> On Sunday November 28 a lad of eleven years of age
> was reading a book at school which another, fifteen
> years old, observing, reprimanded him for, and said,
> the work was unfit to be perused; the boy who was

reading insisted upon the contrary; a scuffle ensued, and the elder of the two got the youngest down, and knelt on him, declaring that he would keep him in that position till he acknowledged the book to be a very improper one to be read; after a struggle, the younger one got the better, and put the other in the same position that he had been in himself. They were soon after interrupted; upon which they agreed to fight it out the next day. They accordingly met on the Monday, and the lad of eleven years of age beat the other so violently that his death was the consequence. The surviving boy now lies in a very dangerous state. The deceased was the son of Mr Wade, an eminent Attorney in the country, the other the son of Mr Masters at Exeter. On Monday night the corpse of the above young Gentleman was interred at Eton College Church. All the Gentlemen of the school attended his funeral.

In March 1825, another dreadful fight occurred, when the Hon Francis Ashley Cooper, aged 15, died after fighting sixty rounds with the fourteen-year-old son of Colonel Wood. Lord Shaftesbury did not prosecute the young Wood, as the fight was according to the rules then general at Eton, but withdrew his other sons from the school. Wood, who nearly died himself, and Ashley's second, who had frequently revived Cooper with brandy between rounds, were both acquitted of manslaughter at the Aylesbury Assizes, because no-one appeared to prosecute or give evidence against them. One wonders what Health and Safety would make of that.

Off to the south-east side of the roadway through College Field is a gateway leading to **Fellows' Eyot**, one of the most beautiful places in Eton. 'Eyot' means 'islet' in Old English, and there are many eyots that remain true islands in the Thames but this one is now largely joined to the mainland.

At the great festivities on the Fourth of June this meadow is thronged with visitors watching the Procession of Boats in which boys wearing the uniforms of Nelson's Navy (coxes as midshipmen, oarsmen as ordinary seamen, but with flowers in their hats) parade past the crowds on the bank, each crew in turn standing with their oars to salute in turn Eton, Windsor and the Queen, shaking the flowers into the stream, first on one side, then on the other and then on both.

Along the track that runs northeast through College Field there is a dense little cluster of favourite Eton places. On the northern edge of the field, heavily shaded by trees, is **Fellows' Pond** (sometimes called The Leg of Mutton from its shape), which is in fact a little appendix of a small stream called the **Jordan** (or the Colenorton

Stream) which runs just north of it. Between the two is a narrow peninsula about a hundred yards long called **Poet's Walk**, said to have been the favourite walk of Thomas Gray.

There has been plenty of rather less contemplative schoolboy life here too. There was skating on the Leg of Mutton in the winter, and it had some wonderful pike in it, which in the nineteenth-century the boys used to angle for with live goldfish as bait, bought from 'a naturalist's shop' in the High Street. Eric Parker, the memoirist of Eton in 1880s, relished exciting adventures in the murky edges of the river:

> Night-lines in the Thames were illegal; but one night-line, at least, was set. It was a line which terminated in six feet of green-stained gut, which was at that time esteemed as better than gut unstained; it was held in the eddies by a flat ledger-lead, painted green, and the bait on a crystal hook was the tail of a carefully cleaned lob-worm. It was set in the meeting of the currents at the corner below Sixth Form bench, in the dusk of a November afternoon; and in the dark of the next morning, a quarter of an hour before early school, it was visited and lifted. And there at the end of it, tugging and fighting, was a large dace. I do not guess at his length or weight,

but he remains the greatest of all dace since taken; he brings back to me, with the grey-green of his scales and the slender shape of him pulling at the green gut in the eddies, the cold and the dark of that November morning, the smell of the river water, the wind blowing on wet fingers and a soaked line. No such dace can be taken before early school by Sixth Form Bench to-day.

But you never know. Only a few years ago, some junior boys fishing for perch, dace or roach off Fellows' Eyot against all probability hooked a salmon and, using an anorak as a net, landed it.

This was the spot where Shelley tried to call up the devil. According to Thomas Jefferson Hogg, his Oxford friend and biographer, Shelley

consulted his books, how to raise a ghost; and once, at midnight, – he was then at Eton – he stole from his Dame's house, and quitting the town, crossed the fields towards a running stream. As he walked along the pathway amidst the long grass, he heard it rustle behind him; he dared not look back; he felt convinced that the devil followed him; he walked fast, and held tight the skull, the prescribed

assistant of his incantations. When he had crossed
the field, he felt less fearful, for the grass no longer
rustled, as the devil no longer followed him.

Three times, he drank the water of the Jordan from the
skull, but no ghost appeared. Perhaps because of these
occult dabblings, Shelley remained haunted for the rest
of his life by 'following figures' whose soft and ominous
tread presaged doom.

Beyond Sixth Form Bench, successive versions
of which have been on this spot since 1625, there is a
tulip tree planted by Queen Elizabeth the Queen
Mother, an Honorary Old Etonian, at the time of her
hundredth birthday in 2000, and an oak commemorating the Queen's Silver Jubilee. The Queen is also an
Honorary Old Etonian – although, as she was taught
constitutional history with her sister by Vice-Provost
Henry Marten, she might well have claimed to be an Old
Etonian in her own right. He often addressed the two
girls as 'Gentlemen'.

On the left across **Sheep's Bridge** are Upper Club, the
Field and Mesopotamia, the heartland at Eton of four of
the five major sports: cricket, rugby, soccer and the field
game. The fifth is rowing, of which more hereafter. Ahead,
across the Datchet Road are the modern running-track

and pavilion, a joint venture with the Local Authorities of Slough and Windsor; the kennels of the Eton College Hunt, built in 1997 to replace the 1899 buildings which were removed to make way for the new flood relief channel, and the hundred and twenty-three acres of playing fields known as **Agar's Plough** and **Dutchman's**. Agar was the nineteenth-century farmer at the moment the fields were saved by Old Etonians and the Fellows from development for housing. Who the Dutchman was remains obscure.

This is so much the world of cricket that Gubby Allan, the O. E. cricketer who had captained England, felt quite comfortable during the Second World War, when on his way to visit his mother in Datchet, about landing a light aircraft here. He was immediately arrested as a spy by the Eton corps. But insouciance was Allan's trademark. In 1929, for Middlesex at Lord's, he took all ten Lancashire wickets for forty runs. A great day's work, but he had done some stockbroking in the City first and arrived at the ground too late to open the bowling.

Cricket was already being played at Eton at the beginning of the eighteenth century, a form of the game in which to get a run the batsmen had to touch the umpire (or at least the long stick he carried). And Etonians were particularly good at it. No Old Etonian XI at Cambridge was defeated between 1758 and 1788.

Upper Club, the most beautiful playing field at Eton, was for long the chief cricket ground, bordered by wonderful elms planted by the Provost in the 1650s. Dutch Elm disease killed them off and the big trees there now are the chestnuts on the eastern boundary. Upper Club is the heartland for the cult of games and colours that swept over Eton as it did over every late Victorian public school. Eton held out against much of that hearty, manly, philistine tide but could not resist it beyond the 1880s and within ten years, as Richard Ollard wrote dismissively,

> the whole apparatus of house colours, school colours and choices sprang into life. From having far too few games it was barely ten years or so before there were too many, taking up too much time and concentrating too much attention....It was of course enthusiastically approved by the vast majority of boys. Indeed it represented an almost perfect expression of puerility. As such it also commended itself to those masters who had never wished to grow up.

At the south-west corner of the cricket pitch, behind the 1860 pavilion with its 1998 addition on legs, a footbridge crosses the Jordan. The other side of the stream is dominated by the so-called **Fifteen Arch Bridge**, which has had three arches since 1833. The bridge is as long as it is to escape the floods which several times a century used to inundate the fields and town. The path diving to the right under the bridge emerges on to the field known as **The Field** in the winter and **Sixpenny** (from the original subscription to its cricket club) in the summer.

Although the Old Etonians won the FA Cup in 1879 and again in 1882, the boys did not play soccer at Eton on a regular basis until it was established in 1930 (when the First XI included the future double-agent Guy Burgess.) Rugby has been popular for the last forty years and in 1993 for the first time more boys opted for rugby than soccer. Originally, Eton played football according to its own laws – at least on the Field. Games played at the other end of the school on South Meadow had their own rules. The 1847 'Laws of the game of football as played in the Field at Eton' describe the field game, a game which is quite like soccer (a round but rather small ball, goals, eleven players) but also like rugby (a scrum called a 'bully', tries called 'rouges') and only like itself, particularly in the moments when three large boys in a 'ram' charged down one small boy standing in the goalmouth, supported by his friends, but with the ball waiting at his feet. Moments of terror never to be forgotten – but also never to be repeated after the decision in the late 1990s that the 'ram' was too dangerous.

In 1845, this was the first place in the world to have a

man on the pitch refereeing a match, if only because the rules, like most public school versions of football, were so arcane. In 1861, the football editor of *The Field* spent half an hour puzzling over them but finally conceded that he could not understand them. Whether Marilyn Monroe, who watched a few minutes of a game on a visit to Eton, was more successful is not recorded.

These rules have been simplified a little (there is some advantage in being the governing body of your own game) and the game is played enthusiastically by most boys in the Lent Half. It has the advantage of being playable in almost any conditions except a flood or deep snow. It is untouched by professionalism and the modern emphasis on excessive levels of fitness. There are no expensive coach trips to matches against other schools. It is played, for fun, between Eton houses, or on Saturdays against as many as eight 'scratches' got up for the purpose by recent old boys. The *Eton College Chronicle* of 1857 had no doubt that games should be fun and deplored the way that 'at Harrow pleasure is subordinated to the science of cricket to an extent which would not be tolerated by Etonians'. Something of that Corinthian spirit survives on the playing-fields of Eton, even in an age when school sport has become almost universally earnest and professionalized.

Rowing, which has some claim to be considered the

greatest of all Eton sports, is taken very seriously by the better oarsmen. Eton's six hundred and eighty Boat Race 'blues' leave Shrewsbury, Radley, and St Edwards several lengths behind, although it has to be admitted that many of them were won in the early years of the race when both crews were likely to be almost exclusively Old Etonians. Eton oarsmen have made sixty-five appearances in the Olympics and won twenty-five gold medals.

The Thames, according to the habitually overstating Hugh Macnaghten, was 'as sacred to the Etonian as Tiber, Father Tiber, was to the Roman of another day.' It is the cradle of English rowing. The row of boathouses and pontoons, known as **Rafts,** a hundred yards above Windsor bridge was the headquarters of Eton rowing until in 2005 most of it was transferred upstream of Brunel's railway bridge (constructed without a central pier to accommodate two crews abreast) to its own rowing lake two miles upstream, the venue for rowing and canoing at the 2012 Olympics. Some recreational rowing still takes place from Rafts and so does the House Bumping Fours competition, which may be the oldest such competition in the world.

It was the inspirational Victorian teacher William Johnson who was ill at Torquay in 1863 and during a sleepless night wrote 'a half-humorous, half-sentimental boating song for the 4th of June'. This was the 'Eton

Boating Song', the paean to the 'jolly boating weather' which seemed to characterize boyhood but nothing afterwards. Lord Rosebery had a scratchy gramophone recording of it played to him on his death-bed and the brass band at Henley belts it out in the middle of each afternoon of the Regatta as the Eton crew paddles up to the start. It lacks the earnestness of most school songs and perhaps it is embarrassingly sentimental. It has a good tune though.

CHAPTER FIVE

THE PRESENT

WHAT IS IT LIKE LIVING and working in these buildings under the shadow of the great men who have passed through them? The first thing to realize is that Eton exists for the boys. This is strikingly illustrated by the five hundred portraits that hang at Eton. The best are the eighteenth and nineteenth-century Leaving Portraits, handsome oils of handsome young men, by Lawrence and Romney, Hoppner and Reynolds. There are modern paintings by Noakes and Brason, Festing, Derek Hill and Foster; and there are dozens of drawings, prints and sketches. A few – but by no means all – of Eton's nineteen prime ministers, have been commemorated and six or seven Head Masters and Provosts have crept in, usually among the drawings, but what is obvious and striking is that the overwhelming majority are of boys.

Most of the time **boys** give very little thought to the buildings or the past. For young Etonians this is just school and the people who matter are the people around them now. By the end of their five years the school hopes that something has stuck, that the sight of brick and stone and green grass on an April morning or scudding clouds across the moon above Lupton's Tower on a wild February night gives them a momentary catch in the breath, but for most of the time their own lives and their own friends are what they care about. They are after all boys.

Two parents wondering whether to send their son to Eton, about which they had some of the conventional prejudices, stopped a small boy in Common Lane to ask his opinion.

> Well, he said, if I were you I would send him.
> Why?
> Well, we're so free here.
> Your uniform looks rather formal. Do you have to wear that?
> Oh, yes. But we're still very free.
> Do you have to play games? – Oh, yes.
> That pile of books you're carrying. Do you have an awful lot of work to do?
> Oh, yes, you don't have much time to yourself, but the great thing here is that when you have time, you're free.

He was in his first year and glorying in his independence. Most schools – and indeed most American universities – make a virtue of communal living in the early years.

Eton makes a virtue of independence. You have your own room, decorated according to your own taste in posters. It is your territory and others come in because you say they can. You have your communal experience in the House and the School, eating together, playing games together and being taught together, but you have your own private space and you do most of your work on your own.

There is no specific time when you have to do 'EWs', your extra work or prep. There are quiet hours but whether you are working, reading, relaxing or gaming is known only to you. It's your business. You can make up your work by getting up early (legally) or after lights-out (illegally). The one certainty is that you will be in trouble in school the next day if you have no work to 'show up'. That is the spur. It's a bit like real life.

Along with independence comes responsibility – not just for your own life but for many of the school's activities. That is risky. If boys run things, mistakes and embarrassments sometimes happen, but having responsibility is the fastest way to learn. Take music as an example. Each year the Precentor, the master in charge of music, appoints one boy as Keeper of the Eton College Music Society. Each term's major school concert and the music competitions will still be the Precentor's responsibility but eight other Music Society concerts will be arranged by the Keeper. He chooses seven other senior musical boys to take charge of one concert each, with total responsibility for the programme to be played, for the organisation of the evening and for persuading the boys needed for each item to agree to rehearse and to play.

One such concert, in which fifty boys took part in the Bach *Magnificat*, was filmed through all stages of rehearsal and performance for *A Boy Called Alex*, a television programme about Alex Stobbs, a boy with cystic fibrosis and a motor-scooter to get him to classes and the music schools. When Alex was rushed to hospital in the middle of rehearsals, television programme or no television programme, no music master took over. It was Alex's concert and his responsibility either to make up time or cancel it. He came out of hospital and it went well.

It is a long-standing tradition that boys run things. In the early nineteenth century, before rowing was officially allowed, it was entirely boy-run. The boys elected as Keeper of the Field in 1954 and 1963 no doubt speak for their predecessors and successors when they recall being in charge, at seventeen, of all the Field Game's internal competitions and fixtures for twelve hundred boys and of dealing with the groundsman. The Beagle Pack has always been the responsibility of the boy elected as Master of the

Beagles for the year. He writes to farmers and landowners to arrange the meets, thanks them afterwards, apologizes if anything goes wrong (when, for instance, hounds run on to White Waltham aerodrome) and arranges for the hounds to be looked after during school holidays. As late as the 1960s masters were still not assigned to football and rugby teams or rowing crews: the boys concerned decided which master they wanted to coach them and the captain invited him by letter. One master, something of a slave-driver on the rugby field, remembers getting a second letter three weeks into the season, informing him politely but firmly that the team had decided to dispense with his services.

The masters-in-charge of each sport now arrange who coaches which school teams but within the House the boy Captain of Games takes total responsibility for arranging matches at all age-groups against the other Houses in football, cricket and the field game. The Housemaster is a benign presence in the background (although it is curious to note that Housemasters who were oarsmen seem to have Houses which row keenly). His roles are only to support and, if one of his teams turns up late or a man short or is guilty of unsporting behaviour, to show his displeasure at the slur on his House's reputation.

It is boys who organize 'House Prayers', the evening House meeting where notices and announcements are supplemented by a reading or a performance by a member of the House. The best musician in the House gets up a choir for the House Singing competition or a House concert for parents. Stephen Layton, Richard Farnes and Edward Gardner showed their flair as impresarios very early. House plays are often directed by a beak, but not always, and the stage-managing, lighting and ticketing are usually boy-run.

There are between forty and fifty Societies at Eton which gather boys of similar interests to hear an expert speaker. It is difficult to be precise about the exact number as they rise and fall phoenix-like as the years pass and interests change, but they include the venerable Political, Film, Debating, Scientific and Equestrian societies and relative newcomers like the Amnesty International, Rock, Entrepreneurship, African and Cheese societies. The important things are that there are close to two hundred invited speakers each year and that it is the boys who run everything. They decide whom they want to hear and write to invite them; they meet them when they arrive, run the meeting and thank them afterwards. The one thing that defeats them is giving guests supper beforehand; so they hone their persuasive skills on Housemasters or other masters who may be induced to provide it. The Political Society wisely has the Provost as patron, which ensures an invitation to the speaker to dinner in the Provost's Lodge.

It is extraordinary how many say yes to an invitation from a boy. 'Provost,' says an apologetic boy appearing at the study door, 'I've come to ask if you could possibly help. The King of Greece has agreed to speak next Thursday and I wondered if you could give us dinner first?'

Both the speaker and those attending the meeting sign the Political Society's book. The boy president writes a brief summary of the meeting the next day. One Old Etonian government minister, signing after his talk, leafed back to a previous visit five years earlier and found that his performance on that occasion had been summed up as 'rather lacking in intellectual content.' He felt lucky, he said, to have been invited back.

On a radio programme Palash Dave the journalist singled out the ability to direct your own play or make your own video as one of the best things about Eton, along with the way it 'allowed, or even encouraged, dissent'. Nick Fraser, on the same programme, thought the ways boys elect their own Society presidents explained something of the Etonian ability to put themselves forward as leaders. They learn early the political arts of being acceptable to the electors. 'What you learn in lessons is quite interesting and useful,' said a boy at the end of his first year; 'but what you learn the rest of the time is more interesting and more useful.'

Boarding has an influence. Day-schools and boarding-schools are alike in offering teaching and games, activities and good intentions, but there are three real differences. The first is that although boarding-schools offer much the same opportunities and activities, there is more time for them. Life is, as one boy put it, 'full on'. The second is that boarding gives you that experience of living alongside people who are not your family which otherwise comes only at university or out in the world. So you learn early how to distinguish the people who are more agreeable or less trustworthy and how to manage both categories. You also discover, not just intellectually but by trial and error, that decency, honesty and fair dealing make for a better society. And very importantly, boarding-schools insert into a boy's life an adult who sees him during term rather more than his mother or father: the Housemaster.

Being a **Housemaster** is the most exhausting, varied, important, fascinating, influential job in schoolmastering. For most boys the House is the quintessential Eton, their home from home, the community within a community to which they belong. So the ideal Housemaster is a *pater familias* who senses when to be intimate and when to be distant, when to encourage and when to rebuke. The Housemaster is considered so important at Eton that while he is in office the House is named after him. The physical building retains its historical name – Mustians, Common Lane, Keate House or Hop Garden – but the fifty boys who use it become McKee's, Graham–Campbell's, Smith's or Jones's. If you ask a boy which House he is in the answer will be 'PJMcK' or 'RDO–C' – his Housemaster's initials. On the touchline at a House match you hear 'Come on, Mowbray's' or even a group chorus of 'Give us a P; give us a J; give us an M. Give us a small C, give us a K'. In later years, if old boys decide to have a dinner, it is not for all those who lived in a particular building in different generations but for those who were there with the same Housemaster. Loyalty is not to bricks and mortar but to a person.

You only become aware of the Head Master or Lower Master (who has a particular care of the youngest two years in the school) when bad behaviour leads you to 'The Bill' (of which more later) or when good work has you sent up for reward. It is the Housemaster who deals with your parents; he consults them and you about your choice of A levels and of university; he is the one who becomes concerned if you are not doing well enough academically and who investigates your misdemeanours. He urges you to make use of your time. 'The thing about my Housemaster,' said one boy, 'is that he insists you should be good at something. He doesn't mind what, but there must be something'.

The first Housemasters at Eton were entrepreneurs who built or bought their own Houses, admitted their own boys and collected their own fees. They were barons of whom the Head Master had to be wary. Over recent decades, however, they have yielded up some of their independence. All Houses are now about the same size, fifty boys (ten in each year) being the right number for one man to look after. Half of the Houses no longer cater for themselves and their boys eat in their House groups in the new dining-rooms in Bekynton. The Bursary collects the fees, sets budgets for the Houses and takes on the bureaucracy of arranging contracts for Dames and domestics.

None the less Housemasters still run their own show and decide on their own House Rules. Most importantly they choose which boys they will take into their House, although no longer at birth. Boys are entered for Eton any time until three years before they are due to come. At eleven they sit the Eton List test and are interviewed by a senior master. About one in three is offered a place provided that he passes the common entrance exam two years later, which he is confidently expected to do. At this point the parents are invited to interview four Housemasters to sound out the possibility of a place in their House and they discover – sometimes to their surprise – that the Housemaster is also interviewing them. Both sides have a choice: the parents have to opt for a particular Housemaster, and the Housemaster, who generally has more applicants than places, has to choose one boy over another. It is a strong bond, to choose and be chosen, and it often leads to friendship as well as to a healthy working relationship. If the Housemaster gets it wrong and has a difficult five years with the boy or his parents, well, it's his own fault.

The European Working Time Directive was not drawn up with Housemasters in mind. During term the Housemaster is never really off duty. He teaches. He lives in the House, just the other side of the study door from fifty high-spirited adolescents for whom, day and night, he is ultimately responsible. Whether he is on-duty or off-duty makes no difference if there is a crisis, an accident or a boy in distress. It is a way of life rather than a job and a married Housemaster requires a wife who at least understands how absorbing it is. As a Housemaster you get to know your boys and their parents. Many find it so interesting and such fun that they do not move on to be headmasters elsewhere. The main qualification for the job, said George Lyttelton, was 'invincible optimism'.

It is to the Housemaster, not to the parents, that the masters teaching a boy send their end-of-term reports on his performance. He sends them on to the parents with a lengthy personal letter, covering everything he thinks needs to be said about the boy's academic progress or lack of it, his other activities and his personality. Perhaps it is easier to be uninhibited when writing to a colleague you know rather than a parent you don't know, or perhaps Eton beaks would write like this anyway:

> A reasonably docile gorilla would have created less disturbance to others and have learned more French than X has done this Half'.

> Y reminds me of my vacuum-cleaner — makes a great deal of noise and picks up very little.

> Lazy, idle and inattentive. Could do better. [Place in Trials: 1st]

> Someone has to come last and he does it with distinction.

Whatever they think about Eton, whether they are for it or against, people generally credit Etonians with the ability to talk. They are not bad at writing either. The report of an A-level History examiner hit the mark:

> As one expects with the Eton candidates the vast majority had no trouble in filling the time and paper available.

The willingness to talk starts with the House. As he goes round in the evening the Housemaster or House tutor drops in on boys in their rooms. There is no escape from a conversation and no-one else is present to tease you afterwards about what you said. So you might as well put the poor man at his ease. Even bad Housemasters have their uses. 'My Housemaster was so impossible to deal with,' says one eminent journalist, 'that I've never had any difficulty since in dealing with anybody.'

The computer – and every boy now has a laptop as once he had a penknife to mend his quill pen – has changed the dynamics of House life a little. Video games vie with passage cricket for popularity and films may be watched by small groups in each others' rooms rather than in a full common room. Email has opened useful new channels of communication but for boys it has one downside: a beak who forgets in school to set work for the next day can now send it round electronically. Since parents reach for their keyboard much more readily than they did for the telephone, Housemasters may spend time answering emails which would otherwise be devoted to going round the House. The sixteenth-century schoolmaster, Robert Mulcaster, wrote that 'parents and maisters should be familiarly linked in amitie and continual conference for their common care.' He now has his wish.

The other person with a tiring, rewarding and vital job in the House is the **Dame**. She looks after all domestic matters from food, clothes and cleaning to pills, sticking-plaster, tea and sympathy. Some are great characters and earn great affection. Douglas Hurd regularly visited Mrs Iredale-Smith, his Matron-in-College, until she died.

Her successor, Naomi Johnston, could have run an empire. She knew what was right, what was wrong and how to cope. On only one occasion she was outsmarted – for a time. Her car seemed to be using a lot of petrol. This led to the discovery that some senior boys were 'borrowing' her car to get up to the opera in London. Had they had the good manners to refill the car, she pointed out, they might have got away with it.

What is it like to teach at Eton? Whether men or women, all teachers are known as '**masters**' or colloquially 'beaks'. (Magistrates in Rome dispensed justice from a rostrum decorated with the beaks or prows of captured ships and that is supposedly the origin of this nickname for magistrates and schoolmasters.) Before the Second World War most beaks were classicists and Old Etonians. A few had been to other well-known schools and most came to Eton from Oxford and Cambridge where a number of them had won Blues. More of them were bachelors than today and several had private incomes. They entertained among themselves and they were good to their boys, whose families often repaid hospitality during the holidays. Although there was less academic pressure in those days, clever boys got a very good deal from these scholar-schoolmasters. Those who wanted to learn were brilliantly-well taught. There were no public exams to worry them: they simply prepared for entry to Oxford or Cambridge. In three successive years around 1971 three Etonians won the blue riband of English academic life, a Prize Fellowship at All Souls.

When Robert Birley arrived as Head Master in 1947 – fresh from reorganizing the educational system in Germany – he resolved to take on at least one beak from a grammar school for every Old Etonian he appointed. 'The only trouble was', he said, 'that ten years later all the grammar-school men had gone off to be headmasters and all the Old Etonians had stayed on.' None the less the pendulum had begun to swing. Looking back on his forty-one years as a historian and later Housemaster, David Evans saw the situation transformed. Old Etonians constitute a small minority of the teaching staff. Now there are only a dozen of them, and less than fifty percent of beaks whose degrees are from Oxford or Cambridge. There are twelve women beaks, and twice as many scientists as classicists. A significant few started life in the city or with university research fellowships and decided to move across in their late twenties or thirties.

The first thing that strikes a new master is the easiness of relationships between teachers and taught. There is very little feeling of us and them. Boys assume that they are all in it together, beak and boys. His job is to teach and theirs to learn but they are after the same goals and on the same side. Even during holidays in far parts boys will cheerfully cross the road to say hello.

Friendship between beaks and senior boys (and often their families) has been characteristic of Eton for more than a hundred years. The bigger change has been in the easy relationship evident these days between younger and older boys.

The more that beaks are involved in organizing games and activities the less responsibility remains to be shouldered by boys, and that is a great loss. However the greater involvement of adults in out-of-school activities has undoubtedly brought boys and beaks closer together. The need for everyone to walk about so much – the school is so spread out that ten minutes has to be allowed between classes – leads to unplanned encounters which make everyone feel part of the same army, although the raised-finger salute known as 'capping' by which beaks and boys wordlessly acknowledged each other as they passed in the street has disappeared in recent years.

Are there as many characters among the beaks? It's hard to say. All boys exaggerate the quirks and eccentricities of those who teach them and the present generation finds plenty to amuse it. Because they coach games, direct plays and visit Houses as House tutors, beaks are known to a lot of boys whom they do not teach in the schoolroom. So their reputation is easily ascertained from another boy in the House, although it may be a partial picture. 'Yes, I know Mr Goode, 'said one new boy. 'He's a really good football coach [of the under-fourteen D team]'. He had no idea that David Goode was also an organist of international standing who had won the organ players' equivalent of an Olympic gold, the performance medal at the Calgary Organ Competition.

Being an Eton beak is certainly not a sinecure. A beak lives in an agreeable place, consorts with agreeable boys and with agreeable colleagues (for the most part, anyway). But he has a trinity of jobs to juggle: teaching, helping with other activities like games, drama and societies, and 'Private Business'.

'Private Business' takes place once a week in the beak's own home with a group of five or six boys to whom he is tutor. The practice goes back to the earliest centuries when boys came to Eton – sometimes from as far away as Westmorland or Northumberland – in the care of a tutor from home who took lodgings in the town, looked after them when they were not in school and helped them prepare their Latin for the next day. In its modern form it is a chance to discuss anything and everything, to introduce books boys would not otherwise read and interests they might never otherwise know existed. To listen to Raef Payne or Archie Nicholson read eighteenth century poetry, to look at pottery with Anthony Ray, the British expert on Delft, or listen to an opera with Charles Impey before going with him to Glyndebourne was education of a different kind from being crammed for an exam. The compulsory modern addition of 'Personal, Social and Health Education' is not quite on the same educational level but has been absorbed into Private Business time.

The school seems determined that Private Business should not become a casualty of the growing emphasis on examinations in the educational world. For many beaks it is still, as it was for David Evans 'the most satisfying and valuable part' of their work. At its best it can be an exciting intellectual partnership; it gives every boy another adult whom he sees regularly and gets to know well, and for some – although it is always a random chance where the spark from Heaven will fall – it can ignite an interest for life.

This is another place where boys make decisions for themselves. They are assigned tutors for their first three years but choose their own for their last two years, by an exchange of letters or, these days, emails. As happened on entry to the school they both choose and are chosen, although this time their parents are no longer part of the equation.

Presiding over this band of clever, individualistic, opinionated and dedicated masters is the **Head Master**. His main job is to appoint the right beaks and to keep them happy most of the time. To be Head Master of Eton sounds very grand and in a way it is. He meets a lot of interesting people and is listened to with a surprising amount of deference. Within the school, though, much of his job is endearingly the same as it was for Robert Birley, Dr Warre and even Dr Keate.

The world known to those great Head Masters of the past has been submerged under a tidal wave of educational legislation, Health and Safety, the Children Act, the Charities Act, examination instructions and the over-regulation of everything, but it has not been totally destroyed. Within the school the Head Master does a number of things that his nineteenth-century predecessors would recognize as familiar. Unlike Keate he probably won't prepare boys for confirmation ('Blessed are the pure in heart.' D'ye hear that, boys: you're to be pure in heart – and if you're not pure in heart I'll flog the lot of you'). But he teaches three or four times a week.

He preaches in Chapel each term. He runs his own Essay Society in his own home. He invites boys to meals. He has a five-minute farewell chat with every boy individually as he leaves at the end of his five years.

Unlike many modern headmasters he is not a remote administrator. He gets around: to watch a few minutes of games, to attend concerts and plays on about fifty evenings a year; to entertain visitors and speak to groups of parents; to chair meetings of the dozen internal committees which run Eton; to represent Eton at educational-meetings in London or abroad; to deal with the media, sometimes as a fire-fighter and sometimes as a columnist. He sees a lot of boys. Most of them succeed in keeping out of his way most of the time, but still he deals personally with hundreds of them each week.

At fixed points in the day you know where to find him. For half-an-hour after breakfast he will be in his study along the Blue Corridor with his door open. Boys with a request for leave of absence, occasionally boys with a problem, boys who have been told to 'show up' an outstanding piece of work, call in to see him. Eton has no annual Prize-Giving. Instead you come for personal congratulations from the Head Master; he signs a prize label and you go off to choose your own book.

At mid-morning it is the turn of the beaks. During 'Chambers', the Masters' Meeting in School Hall at which every beak is expected to be present, notices are read out ('Because of flooding all matches on South Meadow have been transferred to Agar's this afternoon'), explanations given('Apologies that so many boys were late for first school: the visiting speaker in Assembly was difficult to stop'), appeals for help made ('Would anyone be prepared to accompany twenty boys to Wycombe Abbey on Saturday evening for country dancing?') and congratulations passed on ('It will be in the papers tomorrow that Chris Davis has been elected Head Master of Sherborne'). Before and after the announcements beaks move around to catch a word with anyone they need to see, clutching the sleeve of his gown to establish their place in the queue if he is already speaking to someone else. From above, this stately circulation must look like the mating rituals of a tribe of king penguins.

The Head Master spends most of 'Chambers' in earnest talk with one or two Housemasters who have a disciplinary problem that day. Three boys have been smoking again, one has been cutting classes (in Eton's language 'shirking schools') and they have put them 'In the Bill', in other words on the list of those to see the Head Master before lunch.

Boys 'In the Bill' do not go to the study in the Blue Corridor for a pleasant chat. They are seen more formally in the austere surroundings of the Head Master's schoolroom. Two members of Sixth Form (which consists of the dozen cleverest Collegers and the dozen cleverest Oppidans in the top year) assist, one to keep order among those waiting to see the Head Master and one to stay in the room to ensure that justice is done. He has been told to interrupt if he thinks the Head Master is going wrong. That seldom happens but one Head Master was politely told that he was barking up the wrong tree in interrogating a boy to find out who had shared with him the half-bottle of illegally-bought vodka on which he had got horribly drunk. 'What I think you don't realize, sir, is that he is fifteen and bought the vodka for the *purpose* of getting drunk. It's most unlikely he would want to share it with anyone.'

The Housemaster will already have told the tale as he sees it. The Head Master gives the boy the chance to tell his story. Usually the truth comes out and the boy admits it was a fair cop. Occasionally the Head Master has difficulty in keeping a straight face:

> What on earth induced you to act so stupidly and irresponsibly?
>
> 'Sir, Just that I'm an adolescent and won't be much longer'.

Some of these interviews would be hard to make up:

Your Housemaster tells me that your parents are staying at Windsor Castle for Ascot and that you were invited by the Queen to join them for strawberry tea after the day's racing yesterday. You failed to turn up. How on earth did that happen?'

I forgot, sir. After school I went straight off to the tennis courts and it was only when I was throwing up the ball to serve that I noticed the words 'Tea with Queen' on the inside of my wrist. I'd written them there earlier in case I forgot, but I'm afraid I didn't notice them in time.

A difficult letter of apology to write, that one.

'What is a boy?' wrote Tony Chenevix-Trench who was Head Master of Eton in the sixties. 'He is a person who is going to carry on what you have started, to sit where you are sitting and, when you are gone, attend to those things which you think are so important...All your work is going to be judged by him. Your reputation and future are in his hands. All your work is for him, and the fate of nations and humanity is also in his hands. So it might be well to pay him some attention now.'

That is what Masters, Housemasters and Head Master do.

***

For those interested in the business side of running a school, a short addendum to this chapter is needed. Very little of what is described above comes cheap. To finance it Eton has two sources of income: the fees paid by parents and money from its Foundation. About a third of the school fee goes to pay for a boy's academic education, for what happens in the schoolroom. Two thirds is required for everything else, for the facilities for games, art, theatre and music, for the House in which he lives, the meals he eats and the salaries of the people who look after his well-being, day and night, seven days a week.

Boarding-schools are expensive largely because they have to employ so many people. Eton does not help itself in this respect since it offers more subjects than most, more out-of-school opportunities, a single room for every boy, and more care within the House. To cover the same number of classes there are more teachers than at a day-school: since the ethos demands that beaks should also coach games, look after activities, help in Houses and take boys for Private Business, they cannot also teach all the hours there are. Catering, cleaning, laundry, maintenance, libraries, sanatorium, tending grounds and sports fields, providing IT services for two thousand people – along with the necessary accounting and administration – run up a hefty wage-bill. One retiring bursar compared his job with running a resort town with twenty-five small hotels and a university campus.

Henry VI's original endowment, supplemented by occasional benefactions since, provides enough in a good year to pay for the upkeep of the ancient buildings, the care of the collections of books and paintings, and the funding for seventy King's Scholarships, forty Music Scholarships, a dozen Junior and Sixth Form Scholarships and some bursaries. (The notional difference is that scholarships are awarded on merit and bursaries on need, but in fact all are means-tested these days.) The War Memorial Fund to which Old Etonians subscribed in memory of fallen friends, the Camrose Fund and the New Foundation of a further £50 million being raised at present, are devoted to giving bursaries to those who would otherwise be unable to come and defray at least part and sometimes all of the cost of an education at Eton. The Farrer benefaction after the Second World War allowed the school to refurbish some buildings and build others.

Eton is a charity. From the time of Elizabeth I until the Charities Act of 2006 education itself was considered a charitable activity. Now fee-paying schools have to justify their charitable status. Relieving the Exchequer of the cost of educating boys in state schools is not classed as a charitable activity but sharing facilities with the community at large is considered charitable, and so is giving bursaries to needy students. Eton's buildings and sports facilities are used by local clubs, groups and orchestras, and bursaries and scholarships reduce the fees for nearly a fifth of those coming to Eton. In addition the school runs summer schools for young people from all over the country. For nearly thirty years able boys and girls have been helped on their way to Oxford and Cambridge by the Eton Summer School; more than a hundred Eton Choral Courses, during the same period, have brought together young singers from all over the country, and two women Olympic medallists were among the young potential oarsmen and oarswomen who have come to the sport through the twenty years of the Eton Rowing Courses. More recently two inner-London boroughs have been partners in Eton in summer schools for promising sixteen-year olds. All this was happening long before the Charities Act was devised.

CHAPTER SIX

FAMOUS SCHOOL
(FOUR LETTERS)

ETON SUFFER FROM continuous media interest and is invariably the answer to the crossword clue, 'Famous school (4 letters)'. Why? What is it about Eton?

It would be easy to say that the school has prospered over the centuries by keeping the best of the old and adding the best of the new, but that would suggest a guiding principle, a carefully thought-out, settled purpose, which in reality has never existed. What Eton's history illustrates is that it has often been a barometer of society in general, a follower as well as a cautious initiator. It has merely provided, generation by generation, more or less successfully, what people wanted for their boys. Until the mid-nineteenth century the curriculum was almost entirely classics because everyone thought that was the right grounding for an educated gentleman. Now that you need some understanding of science, information technology and modern languages, Eton provides those. Discipline in the eighteenth and nineteenth century was enforced by the strong right arms of boys, beaks and the

Head Master. Modern Eton's disciplinary procedures of detentions, gating and extra work reflect a kinder age. The amount of time spent at home, in chapel and on games and activities reflects the modern consensus on what is best. The standards demanded of boys at school should always be slightly higher than the standards of society at large, but when the winds of change blow, Eton usually changes with them.

Usually, but not always. Twice since the five hundredth anniversary the educational winds have changed dramatically. On the first occasion, when the 1944 Education Act established grammar schools for all who could benefit from them, Eton changed tack accordingly. On the second occasion, when comprehensive schools replaced the grammar schools and secondary moderns, Eton held to its course while state schools veered away.

The grammar schools, which gave a serious academic education to about twenty percent of the population, provided a ladder that any boys and girls of ability could climb, irrespective of where they had started. It was meritocracy in action, rough justice at times, but far and away the most effective tool yet devised for social mobility. They were a challenge to independent schools. They offered the three things that parents wanted: good teaching, out-of-school activities, and discipline. 'No-one but a fool will pay for what he can get for nothing,' says the Chinese proverb, and the grammar schools were free.

So independent schools like Eton had to compete academically. It was no longer enough to concentrate on the cleverest boys; everyone was going to need academic qualifications. The age of earnestness began. It is usually associated with the remarkable headmastership of Michael McCrum between 1970 and 1980 although the foundations were laid by his predecessors. Eton became good at giving every boy what he needed for respectable A level results; almost everyone was equipped to go on to a good university. Edinburgh, Newcastle, Durham, St. Andrews, Bristol and London joined Oxford and Cambridge as favoured destinations, with Harvard, Yale and Princeton attracting a dozen boys a year as well. For McCrum it was not just sensible for Eton to become an academic powerhouse; it was a moral obligation. Etonians had tremendous advantages; they had to justify them by excellence in every field.

Not everyone – especially Old Etonians whose sons failed to get in under the rigorous new dispensation – approved of raised academic entry standards. And they were right in believing that it came at a price. Serious rather than merely recreational music and drama, plus the greater professionalization of school games, at the same time as the rise in academic earnestness: all this crowded the timetable. Gone was the relaxed day with breakfast, chapel, 'Chambers 'and 'After Twelve' punctuating morning schools. Gone was the long languorous Summer Half, now savaged by the educational bodies busy making English schoolchildren the most over-examined in the world (with the exception, it is claimed, possibly fictitiously, of the North Koreans). Even the Fourth of June eventually had to be celebrated on a weekday in late May just before GCSEs, AS-levels and A-level examinations descended to smother the rest of the summer.

When the politicians turned to comprehensive education in the seventies, Eton declined to follow. The comprehensive revolution seemed a denial of all Eton believed in. Previously, Eton had always run parallel to other schools, sometimes better and sometimes worse but offering much the same sort of education. At this point it diverged decisively from the new recommended pattern. Nationally co-education became the norm; Eton remained single-sex. Selection became anathema; Eton, which had traditionally had a fourth-form entry for less clever boys (many of whom however later became highly successful in the City), now selected its pupils on academic merit for the first time. Mixed-ability classes became the fashion; Eton setted rigorously by ability. Competitiveness was frowned on by progressive teachers;

Eton played on the competitive instincts of boys to drive up standards. As the easier qualifications in Media Studies and Combined Science edged out hard subjects such as Modern Languages and Physics elsewehere, at Eton more and more boys took Maths, Physics and, when they became available, Arabic, Japanese and Mandarin.

In the country as a whole much of the received wisdom was turned on its head, with new methods of writing (the abandonment of grammar, spelling and punctuation in favour of 'creativity'), new methods of learning (anything other than learning by rote); new methods of acquiring foreign languages which traded grammar, structure and accuracy for aural proficiency and a lot of guesswork. But at Eton the modern linguists taught grammar even more ferociously than before and two History inspectors, reporting to the Head Master about their day's work, complained that the lessons they had attended were 'rather *didactic*'. 'Oh that's excellent to hear', said the Head Master. 'What else did you think was good?'

By and large the other independent schools did not follow the comprehensive or permissive routes either. So the last thirty years have allowed a comparison between two ways of doing. As independent schools spend more money per pupil than state schools and are dealing with largely middle-class pupils you would expect them to do better on average, and they do. What is remarkable though is that they also do far better by their ablest students whether you measure that by international league tables, A grades in Mathematics, Olympic medals or places at Oxford and Cambridge. The fact that the seven percent educated in fee-paying schools win on merit twenty-five percent of places in the best universities, nearly fifty percent of places in the very best, about forty percent of places in successive Olympic teams and fully half the top grades in hard A levels like Maths requires some explanation.

There would be more than a whiff of special pleading if we were to maintain that this was all due to good schooling. Some of it is. Money, good facilities, supportive parents, an able body of governors, a history to be proud of or a record of success all greatly help a school to be effective. The success of Etonians at Oxford and Cambridge and beyond must have something to do with the pool in which they have been swimming for five years while they acclimatize to the culture, competition and aspiration they are going to meet.

But the advantage of the home environment enjoyed by most Etonians is also massively important: the holiday in Florence, books around the house, the conversation at dinner and the parental expectation of excellence as a normal thing. To be as good as Dad – at least to live a life of which he approves – can be a powerful influence, even the most powerful influence, on how people get on. This is what privilege really is. Those who hate privilege are right in thinking it confers advantages. Privilege is not on the whole money: it is a family culture which holds out excellence as the place where you need to belong.

This kind of privilege is particularly powerful in a meritocracy, where success depends on results. Just as the best ingredients give you the chance to bake the best cakes, the cultural advantages brought from home help schools to produce the best education. That is not to say that the school is unimportant, just that it has a head start. Schools still need to have their own unique ethos, emerging from their particular values and qualities, intangible, difficult to describe and impossible to pin down in a mission statement.

What is Eton's ethos? Previous chapters have tried to give the feel of the place but, as the Introduction says, it is complicated and difficult to define. Perhaps it is possible, however, to suggest five characteristics which contribute to its particular ethos even if they don't add up to defining it. Of course these will please almost no-one. Those who disapprove of selection and competition will be confirmed in their dislike of Eton and schools like Eton. People connected with good schools, state and independent, will claim (quite rightly) that they share more or less the same attitudes and characteristics – so what is all the fuss about? But here goes.

The first characteristic of Eton is that it is – in the proper sense – a selective school. Selection is anathema to people who think it means creaming off the best and caring nothing for anyone else. Actually selection just means choice. A selective school chooses clever pupils or slow learners, dyslexics or gifted musicians, in the belief that the most efficient way to teach is to gather together people of roughly similar talent, ability and willingness to learn. Modern Eton is selective, but not academically highly selective: its boys range in intellect from the top of the scale to marginal grammar-school quality. Most are certainly not geniuses. (One is now an official genius in California, but only one.) On great benefit of selection is that when schools choose their pupils, and in turn are chosen by them and their parents, everyone becomes committed to making a success of the partnership.

A selective school also attracts a small number of very able (and sometimes endearingly individualistic) teachers who might have been university dons, but would simply not want to spend their lives thrusting their subject down the unwilling throats of those who are not interested. Spending their time on discipline and social work has no appeal to them. Passing on their enthusiasm to the next generation has.

A seocnd characteristic is a pervasive assumption that wanting to do well is natural. Most young people are initially reluctant to attempt things they don't know how to do because they don't like making fools of themselves. But aspiration is a pre-requisite of any worthwhile achievement and they have to be persuaded to try. The motto of Gordonstoun has it right: *Plus est en vous*. There is more in most of us than we realize and schools need to encourage it into the light.

> 'What gave you the idea of coming to Oxford?' the professor asks a new arrival.

> It was a teacher in my comprehensive who I didn't really know but who stopped me in the corridor one day and said, 'You know you could get to Oxford if you decided you wanted to'.

Most people need moments like that, but there seems to be no problem at Eton about aspiration. People don't teach it or talk about it. It is simply in the atmosphere, the general assumption that most things are possible or at least not unthinkably impossible. That may be why so many young Old Etonians set up their own businesses.

The doctrine of effortless superiority of the pre-war years is no longer valid and boys don't mind being known to work hard. By the curious alchemy produced by boys in the mass, they seem to have decided that it is cool to be clever and cool to be successful. In earlier generations many jobs went to people who knew people, which meant that just to have been at Eton gave you entry to a powerful network. Nowadays it is different. Most interesting jobs go to people with a good degree from a good university and ability trumps birth and background. Boys on the whole don't think the world owes them a living because they have been to Eton.

The third characteristic, competition, may simply be a corollary to the culture of aspiration. Eton does not subscribe to the view that competition is bad. Life is competitive and school should accustom you to that. So it has become part of the ethos. Twice a year there are internal exams, unappetizingly but accurately named 'Trials'. You are told exactly where you came in every subject. How you do may well put you up or down a set the following term, as Eton believes that the most effective way is to teach people of similar ability in the same room.

Competition is the spur in many out-of-school activities. Getting into each of the dozens of school teams at every age is competitive. House teams compete at most sports in senior and junior leagues fought out by the twenty-five Houses. There are scores of other competitions during the year, some collective like the House Singing or House Drama competitions, some individual like the Declamation Prize or the music competitions in strings, wind, keyboard, singing and bagpiping. Most entrants know they won't win; so it may seem strange that they bother to take part. But in a competitive environment, your own self-respect reuire you to take part. Anyway the truth is that boys enjoy competition. One benefit is that, as you are bound to lose more often than win, you become practised in how to deal with defeat and failure as well as success. One advantage of a big school with a lot of able people in it is that you come to terms with your own level of ability. You don't have illusions about your brilliance, because you have tested that against the others, but by taking a respectable place you prove to yourself that you are good enough. It's a useful discovery.

Fourthly, there is a political element too, and not only in the way boys elect each other to office and learn the arts of appealing to their electorate. Eton is not a place of centralized control and its command structure is a subtle and shifting thing. If you can talk well, absorb a brief, concentrate under pressure, grow a thick enough skin to take criticism and persuade others to follow your lead there are plenty of hierarchies at Eton to scramble up. When little is laid down, the key talent, if things are to go the way you want – the central political skill – is the ability to negotiate. Courteous negotiation produces rewards, and so boys develop the ability to bring people together, to accommodate difference and to make things happen, a package of skills that defines the modern Etonian and which often goes under the label of Etonian charm.

The final element that goes into the making of the ethos – an element which can only be supplied by the enthusiasm of those who teach – is the awareness that there is more to education than exams. Most intelligent young people are happy enough to do the work and get the qualifications, but school should give them glimpses of a world beyond the humdrum, in A.N.Whitehead's words, 'the habitual vision of greatness'. If schools do not introduce the young to some of the great men and women of history, to some of the exciting discoveries of science and the big moral questions, to the elegance of mathematical solutions, to the words of Shakespeare, Molière and Cervantes, to the art of the Renaissance, to the best that has been said and written and done, these worthwhile things will probably pass them by for ever. In a world seemingly dedicated to trivialities, good schools, Eton among them, are in the front line of the battle for quality.

Today's Eton is not the same as pre-war Eton, let alone the Etons of Gladstone, Charles James Fox or Henry Wotton. The royal Founder would, however, recognize the college buildings he provided for the 'Lady mother and mistress of all other grammar schools,' and would be pleased that through the changes and chances of five hundred and seventy years it was still faithful to his intention of bringing up boys in goodness to become 'honest citizens, useful to their country.'

www.longbarnbooks.com

SIMS HALL   MITFORD
A.G.
L.COOKESLEY   H.W.R.
K.SWEETLAND
HERBERT   H.M.NOR
BLAIR R.D.CARTER W.
SHAW
PIERCE STEWART
CAMPION H.P.STUR
ARBUTHNOT R.W.
UPTON H.N.STURT
G.WEDDERBURN
M.FARQUHAR
S.WADDINGTON
TOTTENHAM H.S.
W.MILES E.N.RIGHT
W.MILES J.R.V.ES